CONTEMPORARY CHRISTIAN MUSIC . . . IS *THAT* IN THE BIBLE?

Oh, Be Careful Little Ears

Kimberly Smith with Lee Smith

WINEPRESS WP PUBLISHING

Oh, Be Careful Little Ears
Copyright © 1997 by Kimberly A. Smith
First edition printed: 1997
Second edition printed: 2000

Printed in the United States of America

Published by:
WinePress Publishing
PO Box 428
Enumclaw, WA 98022

Cover by **DENHAM**DESIGN, Everett, WA

Unless otherwise indicated, all Scripture references are quoted from the King James Version of the Bible or, as noted, from the New American Standard Bible, with permission from The Lockman Foundation.

ISBN 1-57921-045-7
Library of Congress Catalog Card Number: 97-61414

ACKNOWLEDGMENTS

I'd like to thank the following people who have had a part in this book—either by praying, discussing, editing, or encouraging. I appreciate each of you.

Pastor Gary and his wife Sharon; my mother and stepdad; Robert and Delores; Diana; Connie; Karen; my ladies' Sunday School class; and the wonderful people at Highland View Baptist Church. (See Proverbs 27:17.)

A special thank-you to Dr. Frank Garlock for his kind encouragement; "Little Bear" Wheeler for his counsel; David J. De Simone for his help and information; and Chuck Dean for his suggestions.

Last, but foremost, a *huge* thanks to my family for their patience, and especially to my husband, Lee, without whose support and wisdom this book would have never become a reality.

CONTENTS

IN SPIRIT AND IN TRUTH

Just because something is "legal" doesn't make it morally right. "Political correctness" is not always "correct." Change is not always for the better, yet neither does the statement, "We've always done it that way," make a practice valid.

The last few decades of the twentieth century have certainly seen changes in Christian music, and these changes have resulted in a polarization of God's people. Because these changes are accepted by many, does that make them right? Are the old ways the *only* ways?

The subject of Christian music is controversial—probably one of *the* most controversial areas in Christian circles. Undeniably, if Satan can get us fighting about anything, our witness for Christ will be negatively impacted.

Can we lay aside our differences and "reason together" for a little while? It's time that *all* of us took a serious look at Scripture, and if we've made mistakes, we should be honest enough to admit to them. If we have been correct, we should be merciful. And above all, each of us should demonstrate Christ's love to one another.

What is the truth concerning music? Music is an expression of ourselves. That expression needn't be suppressed—just molded to conform to Godly standards set forth in Scripture. Just as we must accept Jesus Christ as our personal Savior (God's provision), we must also accept God's provision and direction in Scripture concerning our music.

Throughout this book our thoughts about music are going to be "tested and tried." We'll want to remain in our "comfort zone." We may even find ourselves pleading with God: "What *is* right concerning music? I *know* I've heard Your voice—music that seems acceptable to me *ministers* to me!"

Self-examination is beneficial and essential if we're to "grow" in Christ Jesus. It's a continual process. When one layer is "peeled away," another is there waiting to be peeled away. Yet, avoidance of scriptural evaluation in any area hinders a *deeper* relationship with Jesus Christ.

Music seems to be a "gray" area, and we measure its effectiveness by the response it brings forth. For example, we can certainly "fill the pews" and put on a great song service. People will clap and sing and comment about how great the music is. However, in comparison, which gets more "amens"—our "special music" or the Word of God boldly proclaimed? Have we put more emphasis on our music than on life-changing messages from Scripture? Have we un-knowingly—yet with good intentions—allowed "sin in the camp"? Can music really be evaluated? Yes, and clearly so.

Oh, Be Careful Little Ears has been written out of a deep concern for God's people, a desire and burden that we re-member *His* holiness and direction from Scripture in our music, as opposed to what *we* want to hear—both in our worship services and in our personal lives.

At times its message may be strong, even "radical," but it's a message we need to hear. A message that, surprisingly, fifty years ago would have been commonplace in our pulpits. Has God changed? No, *we* are the ones who have changed, who have fallen into the snare of "doing what is right in our own eyes" concerning music.

Are we ready for this message? Can we strip away our pride and pre-conceived ideas concerning music and really *see* what Scripture has to say? Will we ask the Holy Spirit to show us the truth concerning music?

It's my prayer that through this book each one of us will be led to a deeper walk with the Lord Jesus Christ, a walk that will be manifested through music that truly honors Him "in spirit and in truth,"[1] and that will result in a personal renewal—in our hearts, in our churches, and in our land.

May God bless each of you,
KIM

CHAPTER ONE

CAN YOU HEAR THE BEAT?

"For the time will come when they will not endure sound doctrine; but after their own lusts shall they heap to themselves teachers, having itching ears."

II Timothy 4:3

A nation watched, shocked, yet mesmerized, as he "gyrated" on the national television broadcast of an Ed Sullivan show. The teenagers loved the controversy; the adults were offended. The year: 1956. The performer: Elvis. A new musical culture was born.

Fast-forward to the 1990s. Those teenagers are now grown with children of their own, and Elvis's performance seems laughable. Why? Our "line" between what we consider "acceptable" and "unacceptable" music has *moved*.

It's obvious to most people that certain music is evil. It's not so obvious where we draw a line to determine what is okay and what isn't. In fact, the "line" will be different for each and every individual. And what about contemporary Christian music? Are the rules different?

Yes, we can hear the "beat" in any and all rock music.* In rock music, a drum, percussive device, or bass guitar plays the noticeable "beat," which creates an "unnatural" rhythm that conflicts with ("fights" against) the melody. *It is an entity in and of itself,* and this is what distinguishes rock music from most other types of music.

This "fight" between the beat and the melody is analogous to the war within the Christian between his fleshly (carnal) self and his spiritual (non-carnal) self. And herein is the dilemma: If we're to succeed in our spiritual lives, if we're to *"walk in the Spirit"*[1] and *"make not provision for the flesh, to fulfill the lusts thereof,"*[2] can we use rock music to that end? Can perpetuation of this spiritual conflict through the music we listen to bring us to victory to the glory of God?

As we will see in chapter five, unnatural rhythms create sensual sounds and, therefore, "carnal" music, no matter what the words—Christian or otherwise. Because of the carnal nature of the music—like it or not—"Christian" rock is a *compromise.* How can it be anything else? Moreover, it will be shown in chapter four that the Christian is exhorted to sing "spiritual *[non-carnal]* songs"[3] to edify himself and other believers.

Why is the beat carnal?† We'll see in the next chapter that the beat came out of a pagan (godless) culture. A pagan, by definition, is one who is not spiritually minded but responds to the flesh. Romans 8:7 says, *"Because the carnal mind is enmity against God: for it is not subject to the law of God,* neither indeed can be" (emphasis added). So, in essence, the pagan has developed rhythms *that will please his flesh.* This is evidenced by *our* reaction to certain rhythms as well. Turn on the radio and analyze different types of music (rock, classical, march, etc.). *If the music causes your body to move in a way that could be construed as sensual or suggestive or, to be more precise, causes you to want to "thrust out" your head, shoulders, or hips—or even tap your toes— "in time" to an additional, identifiable "beat," it is appealing to the flesh.* This isn't to be confused with the straightforward "toe-tapping" response, as in a march, which is usually to *every* beat of the melody's rhythm. The *difference* in our body's response is an indicator of whether the music is appealing to our "flesh" or to our spirit. If you have any doubt, exaggerate your body's response to the music (make the movements more pronounced). Is your body's response a "clean" response to the *melody* (the part we hum), or is your body responding to an *additional* percussion or bass guitar beat?

Are we ready to do some honest soul-searching? Are we, by listening to rock music—secular or Christian—following God's Word that commands: *"But put ye on the Lord Jesus Christ, and make not provision for the flesh, to fulfill the lusts thereof"* (Romans 13:14)?

I can understand that some would consider "Christian" rock much better than the alternative—secular rock. But isn't that looking at the situation from a worldly perspective and giving it an *incomplete* evaluation? We must understand as Christians that we aren't limited to those two choices.

My son attended a Christian meeting once where Christian rock was played at one point. He said he could catch only a word here and there, and what was worse, one boy made gestures like he was playing a guitar in a rock band (complete with sunglasses). Is this the spiritual response that Christian contemporary rock singers are supposedly striving to evoke from their listeners?

A line *has* to be drawn somewhere, and the obvious place to draw it is at the unnatural rhythms—the beat—however subtle, in rock music. Any rock music. To draw it anywhere else is totally subjective, because *my* "line" will not be *your* "line." So then, *"Can two walk together, except they be agreed?"*[4] As we saw in our Elvis example, the line *moves* because what a person listens to he learns to like, and that's what he wants to hear. We *can* learn to like music other than that which has a beat. It's just a matter of deciding what's important to us: listening to the beat or following scriptural principles.

Those of us who witnessed the ushering-in of rock music at some point in our lives had a natural disinclination for the rock beat. But after we heard it time after time, it wore us down, until finally it was acceptable. Our ears became attuned to the unnatural rhythms, so the "unnatural" became "natural" to us.

We became desensitized and after awhile we needed something a little stronger to "satisfy the flesh." If today we were to listen to the rock music that was played in the late 1950s and early 1960s, we would call it "tame." Back then it was considered "shocking," yet those who have grown up not knowing the difference readily accept today's rock music and continue to stretch its boundaries.

In his book, *How to Listen to God*, Charles Stanley states:

"...[Satan] comes in the backdoor using the most cunning, convincing, persuasive language possible.

*The best way in the world to deceive believers is to
cloak a message in religious language* and declare that
it conveys some new insight from God."[5]

Is this what has happened to the music in our churches?

Chapter One Notes

* Throughout the remainder of this book, the terms "rock" and "rock
music" will be used to cover the entire spectrum of music that came
out of the rock movement, including, but not limited to, the following:
soft rock, country rock, punk, rap, heavy metal, grunge, and that all-
inclusive term, "alternative." All of these examples contain unnatural
rhythms, a term that will be more fully explained in chapter five but
which, in a nutshell, means "unnatural" to the Christian's way of living.
† The "beat" is only one of several carnal musical techniques. See chapter five.

CHAPTER TWO

THE ORIGINS OF UNNATURAL (CARNAL) RHYTHMS

"For the wisdom of this world is foolishness with God. For it is written, He taketh the wise in their own craftiness."

I Corinthians 3:19

NOTE: This chapter is certainly not intended to point fingers at any particular culture. We *all* are sinners, and we *all* need Jesus Christ as our Savior. However, the history of rock music's development cannot be denied, and while the rhythms of one culture were pagan (though innocently so originally), the rebelliousness of the other culture, which was not so innocent, is what provided the catalyst for rock music.

I could feel the war within myself as the complex rhythms of the drums and chants drew me into their spell: a war between my body's need to respond to the beat, and my mind and spirit's rejection of what was, indeed, "carnal" music in its purest form. As I experienced this reenactment of slave music from the 1700s,[1] I realized that this was one of several confirmations of everything God had shown me through my research. It was also confirmation that the "beat" did not originate with rock music.

Although many people attribute the beginnings of rock 'n' roll to somewhere around the early 1950s in this country, its actual *roots* go back much farther—all the way to Africa.[2]

Music was important to the African. It seems that every facet of life was set to music.[3] Foundational to their music was rhythm, "...the basic pulse upon which the music is built...strong and constant."[4] Add to this diverse syncopation, played with a multitude of percussive instruments, plus dissonance in the melody and harmony, and we have the basis of African music.[5]

This strong musical heritage went with them wherever they were transplanted and settled, and it influenced the music of all the countries in which they have lived.[6]

In America in the seventeenth and eighteenth centuries, the Africans found emotional release in singing. It was "one of the few expressions allowed them."[7] As men labored, work songs and early "blues" emerged. In much of the South, east of the Mississippi River, drums, which were so important in Africa, were banned. Nevertheless, the early African-Americans invented other percussive devices out of materials available to them.[8]

The African was a master of improvisation, and this was evident in his ability to turn hymns he heard the white man sing into what we now know as "spirituals."* 9 10

As the Africans learned and adopted Western culture music (European melodies and harmonies), they added their own flavor to it with improvisation and enlivened rhythms. White men were attracted to this new style and began to imitate it in the early part of the nineteenth century.12

During this time a more lenient attitude existed in the territory of Louisiana, particularly in New Orleans. This city was prosperous, with foreigners from all over the world coming and going. Drums were not banned there, and voodoo was practiced as a religion.13

Following the Louisiana Purchase, because many primitive forms of dancing were then forbidden, the Africans formed their own bands, after the example of Napoleon's military band. These bands played at funerals to honor their dead (a practice which stemmed from ancestor worship), and out of this Black marching bands became popular. Although they played the familiar tunes of the day, they did so with their own improvisational flair that "...reached a state of perfection toward the end of the century that still survives as the hallmark of classic jazz."14

Toward the end of the 1940s a new type of culture began to emerge. The word "teenager" came into being, and white musicians combined elements of boogie-woogie, blues, and jazz to form a new kind of music.15

In addition to this, disc jockeys played "race records," having rediscovered the "original, robust style" of the black jazz musicians.16

"The contemporary style, with a name derived from a combination of two words long ago used in Negro folklore,

21

rock 'n' roll, became the most controversial popular music ever to have hit this country."[17]

And controversial it was. Played almost solely by white musicians in those early days, "the music was sensual and rhythmic...steeped in rebellion."[18] Through the years its style has evolved and changed, yet "its roots are Afro-American."[19]

As we have just seen, the African influence on music came out of a culture of pagan beliefs and practices. In contrast, the music of Western culture began with the early Church, as we will see in chapter six. Interestingly, after the Africans were converted to Christianity, they expressed their new Christian faith in a worship style that embraced freedom of movement during their services. This, *in their cultural context*, could not be considered "wrong." (NOTE: Their spirituals weren't accompanied by instruments.[20] More on cultural uniqueness in chapter eleven.)

However, the basic unnatural rhythms—the carnal "beat"—together with the *intent of rebellion* which was the catalyst of "official" rock 'n' roll, *are* wrong.

How ironic. African-Americans, after conversion to Christianity, took their pagan musical heritage and turned it into beautiful and uplifting spirituals. Conversely, white men, whose musical foundations are "Christian," have rebelliously taken the pagan rhythms of the African culture and "married" them to Western civilization's music—forming "rock" music.

Even though we have been desensitized and each of us has moved the "lines" regarding what we consider "rock" music, we still can't deny the truth. Simply defined in *The World Book Encyclopedia*, most rock music has "a strong *beat* with off-beat accents and repeated harmonic patterns" (emphasis added).[21]

Because of this "marriage" with pagan rhythms, Christian rock music (which includes quite a lot of contemporary Christian music) is certainly not the best we have to offer God, as we shall see in the following chapters.

Chapter Two Notes

* "White" gospel/Southern gospel music, which originated in the South during the 1800s, was influenced by the spirituals and "black gospel" music. (Black gospel was much more spontaneous and emotional than white gospel.) D. L. Moody and Ira D. Sankey exposed large audiences to gospel *hymns* at white revivals.[11] The original gospel hymns were hymns that simply shared the Gospel's message through personal testimony, and are different from most music we call "gospel" today.

It's important to note that there's a major difference between unnatural rhythms and the syncopation used in some traditional, four-part gospel music (not gospel hymns). (See chapter five.) Gospel's syncopation has a "clean" sound in that the response it evokes is "toe-tapping" or "knee-slapping," similar to that evoked by a march. It could almost be classified as a type of folk music. This is unlike the sensual (carnal) response one feels when hearing unnatural rhythms and/or other sensual sounds. But be aware: much contemporary gospel music—both "black" and "white"—does make use of these carnal devices. (A little discriminatory listening will bring these differences to light.)

For the most part, traditional, old fashioned, four-part gospel music is "good, clean fun," and has value as uplifting *entertainment*, and most definitely the traditional gospel *hymns* have a valid place in our worship services.

CHAPTER THREE

WHERE HAVE ALL THE HYMNS GONE?

"Rock of Ages, cleft for me,
Let me hide myself in Thee."[1]

NOTE: This chapter is a simplified overview of the development of hymns. Across the centuries, hymn-singing practices varied according to denomination (Catholic, Anglican, Lutheran, Moravian, Baptist, Methodist, Presbyterian, etc.). To attempt to examine each denomination's hymn singing practices would be overwhelming.

A simple hymn, "Amazing Grace," played by a lone bagpiper at a friend's funeral poignantly captured both the meaning of passing from life on earth to life in heaven, and the *reverence* of Almighty God. It's times like these—when we're faced with the reality that life on earth is brief—that we understand in our spirits the *holiness* of God and the seriousness of the choices we make during our life on earth.

We've lost that "reverence" in many churches today because, unfortunately, the clutter of much modern-day music doesn't aid a person in finding a stillness in his soul where he can hear God's voice. Regrettably, many churches are abandoning the traditional hymns in favor of "contemporary" music or, to be more exact, "praise" music. This presents a problem, because hymns are important for several reasons.

The word *hymn*, or *hymns*, appears only in the New Testament, and according to the Greek, by implication, means "to celebrate God in song; i.e., sing a religious ode."[2]

Ode is an unusual word in our day, but it is simply defined as "A lyric poem often addressed to a praised object or person and characterized by exalted style."[3]

The early Church used the Psalms as hymns. Centuries passed, new hymns were written as poems, and later these were set to simple, unaccompanied melodies. Often the music, or "hymn tune," was written by a different person.[4] Early practices in congregational hymn singing involved a church "clerk" who would "line out" (read or sing a line of a hymn). The congregation would echo him, continuing this pattern throughout the entire hymn, line by line. In some churches this practice continued through most of the eighteenth century.

From the Reformation until the eighteenth century, most hymns were Psalms or paraphrased Psalms, and Protestant denominational differences dictated congregational singing practices. Some (particularly the German-speaking churches) adopted Martin Luther's four-part chorale music; others (the French and English Protestants) preferred

John Calvin's more conservative ideas and kept the method of "lining out" the hymns, sometimes to no particular tune.[5]

Then along came Isaac Watts (1674–1748), an English clergyman, who:

> "...insisted that in confining songs of praise to the Book of Psalms, the worshipper was behaving as if Christ had never been born, had never died, and had never been raised from the dead and 'received up into glory.'"[6]

He argued that Christian praise lacked New Testament content, and he persevered to supply that lack,[7] publishing a hymnbook in 1707. His hymns, like many early hymns, were sung ("lined out") to already existing tunes familiar to the Christians at that time.[8]

What Isaac Watts did was "complete the picture" of religious hymns. He *completed* what was already in existence— the Psalms—by adding more than seven hundred hymns and Psalms about Christ.[9]

With the Methodist Movement came Charles Wesley (1707–1788), who greatly helped to bring about this change in hymnody by writing more than seven thousand hymns.[10] Through the years many other men and women have contributed inspired verses, and all denominations now share in the legacy of numerous beautiful, meaningful hymns.

Many early hymnals were commonly considered books of poetry since they contained only the words of songs. The people knew certain hymn tunes, so the minister would choose a hymn-poem and announce the tune to which it would be sung.[11] Of course, today our hymnals have both the words and music, harmonies have been added over the years, and we've come to associate certain tunes with specific hymns, and vice versa. So, to us the words and music of each hymn are synonymous.

It must also be noted that the simple, harmonious melodies of traditional hymn tunes contain orderly, straightforward rhythms[12] which, by their very nature, do not appeal to our flesh, but help us direct our attention to the meaning of the words.

Why are hymns important? Focusing on traditional hymns during worship provides continuity from one generation to the next, and it's comforting to know that God's people have sung the same hymns throughout the ages. Furthermore, if contemporary music continues to *dominate*[*] our worship services, the timeless beauty and wisdom of the hymns will be lost and, sadly, our youth will be deprived of knowing the wonderful old hymns.

Something else to consider is the fact that the Christians who wrote the hymns down through the centuries were influenced by those men of the faith who had gone before them, each one closer to the time when Jesus walked the earth.

Therefore, we must prevail in handing down the faith that has been handed down to us through the centuries. We *must* pass this same faith down to the generations to come, and traditional hymns are a beautiful and meaningful way of doing this. They're rich in Bible truths and help to establish a peace in our worship services.

Moreover, if we abandon the hymns, with their edifying influence, in favor of "contemporary" music, we are, in effect, saying, "It's okay to adapt the Church, through its music, to the culture of the time." The Church then becomes like a chameleon, changing its color to adapt to the color of the world. In other words, we're letting our culture influence our religion, rather than, as Christians, positively influencing our culture by being the "salt of the earth."

Chapter Three Notes

* There is a *place* for *meaningful* contemporary praise music in our worship services if the music itself is *non-carnal*. See chapters four and five for more information.

CHAPTER FOUR

BIBLICAL REFERENCES TO MUSIC

"Study to show thyself approved unto God, a workman that needeth not to be ashamed, rightly dividing the word of truth."

II Timothy 2:15

"Oh, be careful little ears what you hear." Most of us have sung that little verse as children and usually associated it with the spoken language—words that are kind instead of hurtful. The verse taught and encouraged us to be careful to guard what we allowed ourselves to hear.

Then we became adults, and who knows *what* we hear on a daily basis. As Christians, we're offended when we hear certain words or phrases, but we've also become *desensitized* to many other things we hear. One of those things is music because of its constant barrage on our senses everywhere we turn in the secular world. As a result, we lose our discernment in this area. Does it matter? Is music that important?

The answer has to be yes, because half of our worship services consists of music. Take music from our daily lives and there is a vast void.

In the Old Testament book of Deuteronomy, God warned the Israelites many times to "take heed," "be diligent," "be careful" for their souls.[1] We might say, "Well, that applied to the nation of Israel, not to us." However, the New Testament says that their example is *"written for our instruction…Therefore let him who thinks he stands take heed lest he fall."*[2] Aren't we all human? Aren't we *all*, like the Israelites, capable of being influenced by most anything? As the old hymn says, we're "prone to wander."[3] We *all* must be diligent for our souls.

So why worry about Christian music? We are, after all, praising God with meaningful lyrics. Doesn't God "inhabit our praises"?[4]

But *what if* we have become so desensitized to the musical realm that we have actually accepted unacceptable music into the church? *What if* we have not remained diligent to guard our souls—or our ears—and have allowed wrong music into our lives? We've seen in previous chapters that some music is carnal, but is that alone enough proof that some music is wrong for the Christian? If we add Christian lyrics, won't the carnal nature of the music be negated? And does the Bible *really* give any direction about our music?

Two categories of music are referred to in the Bible: religious and secular.[5] This chapter will deal specifically with religious music. Another chapter, "A Word About Pop Music," will deal with secular music.

It's difficult to pinpoint specifics about the type(s) of music we're to sing to the Lord. Most references, when researched further in the original Hebrew and Greek, mention only singing, or singing to the accompaniment of instruments. Sometimes the Bible says to sing loudly, sometimes to sing joyfully. But there's no seemingly clear-cut reference to the actual *kind* of music that's to accompany our singing.

After an exhaustive search of music, psalms, songs, singing, and associated words concerning music, we *do* find two related verses in the New Testament which indicate the type of music we should sing to the Lord:

> *"Speaking to yourselves in psalms and hymns and spiritual songs, singing and making melody in your heart to the Lord."*
>
> Ephesians 5:19

> *"... Teaching and admonishing one another in psalms and hymns and spiritual songs, singing with grace in your hearts to the Lord."*
>
> Colossians 3:16

In these verses we notice three different kinds of music: Psalms, which are self-explanatory; hymns, discussed in the previous chapter; and "spiritual songs." Why would Paul also indicate "*spiritual* songs" when the other two are so clear? Because, though the early Christians were free to use music in their worship services, there was certain music in their culture he did not want them to imitate. Hymns were also used by pagans in their heathen worship,[6] but evidently this "style" was acceptable so long as the words glorified God. When Paul told the early Christians (and us) to sing

33

"spiritual songs," we can surmise that some forms (or styles) of music that the pagans used were not acceptable for use in the Church. Why?

The phrase "spiritual songs" means any music and words, apart from psalms or hymns, with a qualification: *Spiritual*, translated from the Greek word *pneumatikos*, means "non-carnal," and in these instances refers to the higher or renovated nature.[7] This is our new nature as Christians.

In other words, we're to sing *non-carnal* songs. The obvious and superficial interpretation here is that the words of a song should edify the believer. Yet there has to be more: When Paul gave direction to sing "hymns" (a pagan practice), it must have been understood that the words should be glorifying to God. Paul didn't have to qualify them as "spiritual hymns." Evidently, some other "types" of music in their culture were *not* acceptable to imitate by only supplying different words, hence the qualifying "spiritual" (songs). Otherwise, the phrase "to the Lord," which occurs at the end of these verses, would have been sufficient. The book of Ecclesiastes tells us there is nothing new under the sun, so we can't assume that all music in Paul's time was "simplistic." On the contrary, history shows us that early Christians did not imitate nor tolerate other forms of secular music, and that early Church music was solely vocal (as opposed to the secular music of that period).[8] (See chapter six.)

Therefore, the interpretation and application of the word "spiritual" (non-carnal) would indicate that the Christian's music should be both non-worldly (meaning different), and non-carnal (meaning that it nourishes the renewed spirit and does not stir up nor appeal to our old, carnal sin nature). And knowing Paul, who so stressed a denial of our sin nature, he most likely would have been careful to direct the early Christians to musical forms which would nurture their new life in Christ—as opposed to carnal music which would encourage their old habits. In light of this, "non-carnal" (spiritual) songs *must* refer to both the music and the words.

This is an area that we've neglected in the last half of the twentieth century, and unquestionably, we've allowed carnal music into the Church, having misinterpreted "spiritual songs" to mean that *any* form of music is acceptable if the words glorify God.

We may think we're being edified by the words of a Christian song—and certainly some contemporary lyrics are outstanding in their message. But we need to take this a step further and evaluate the music itself. *It is the music that is the vehicle for those words.* Does the vehicle *match* the message of the lyrics, or does it *contradict* the message because it's carnal? Is the vehicle encouraging our lives to be more Christ-like, or encouraging us to be more world-like? And finally, if you remove the lyrics, does the music command the listener's respect and direct his or her attention toward a living, powerful, Almighty God?

We have basically three choices concerning music: The first two choices are carnal music and spiritual (non-carnal) music. Carnal music, as we've seen, is music which appeals to our flesh through unnatural (improper) rhythms and/or other sensual devices.* It may or may not contain lyrics. Spiritual music ("pure" music with a straightforward melody and no additional obtrusive rhythms or other sensual techniques) appeals to our spirit and glorifies God.[9] It also may or may not contain lyrics. Obviously, when we are told to "speak" in "spiritual songs," there will be lyrics involved that will edify the believer and glorify God.

Now, can we take these two opposite concepts—carnal and non-carnal—and mix them so that, in effect, we have "carnal/spiritual" music? This would be music that appeals to the flesh through unnatural (carnal) rhythms and/or other sensual devices and is "married" to lyrics that are spiritual. Would this be a valid fulfillment of the instruction to sing "spiritual songs"?

Lyrics that aren't spiritual yet don't compromise our Christian values could be considered non-carnal/non-spiritual lyrics. And when they are added to good music, we have a third choice in music: non-carnal/non-spiritual (for example, the songs in *The Sound of Music*).

Worldly (carnal) lyrics[†] set to otherwise good music make the music carnal. But it is not true that spiritual lyrics set to carnal music make the music spiritual. It is *still* carnal. Look at the following diagram:

	Spiritual music (S)	Carnal music (C)
Spiritual lyrics (S)	S/S	S/C
Carnal lyrics (C)	C/S	C/C
Non-carnal lyrics/ Non-spiritual lyrics (N)	N/S	N/C

Unquestionably, *only one* combination is truly spiritual music as a fulfillment of Ephesians 5:19 and Colossians 3:16 and is worthy to be offered to a Holy God. In *every other* combination the *lowest* standard gives the music its value as carnal or non-carnal/non-spiritual music.

Now that we have clear direction concerning non-carnal (spiritual) music, it stands to reason that if we continue to sing and/or listen to any music that is carnal, we disobey Paul's exhortation to *"make not provision for the flesh, to fulfill the lusts thereof."*[10] By allowing ourselves to listen to such music, we've made a decision and, in actuality, are saying, "This is *my* music; this is an area that doesn't need to be surrendered to the Lord." Or we might say, "God knows my motives; my heart is pure." Yet, either way, we *have* made provision for the flesh, and are setting ourselves up for spiritual conflict.

Proverbs 6:27 states: *"Can a man take fire in his bosom, and his clothes not be burned?"* In other words, sooner or later the carnal music *will* affect us—whether it's set to Christian lyrics or not. It may affect us greatly, or only subtly, but affect us it will, and it will not be to encourage us to become more like Christ.

Does the lack of further biblical examples give us license to use music in a way that pleases us? No. Hebrews 5:14 indicates that mature Christians must be able to discern (judge) things as either good or evil, and music cannot escape this evaluation. For every single issue in life that isn't *directly* addressed in Scripture (for example, abortion and gambling) God has given us *biblical principles* that *can* be applied. (We'll be looking at some of these principles in later chapters.) To disregard these principles is a serious mistake, for we *will* be held accountable.

"For we must all appear before the judgment seat of Christ; that every one may receive the things done in his body, according to that he hath done, whether it be good or bad."

II Corinthians 5:10

Chapter Four Notes

* Unnatural rhythms and sensual devices will be defined in chapter five.
† Worldly lyrics promote a message contrary to scriptural teachings. For example: adultery, drunkenness, rebellion, immorality, etc.

CHAPTER FIVE

THE MUSIC VEHICLE:
CARNAL OR NON-CARNAL?

"Blessed are the peacemakers…"
Matthew 5:9

A young singer captivated the audience through vocal techniques and subtle body movements that matched the music's underlying rhythms. The crowd's approval became evident as they joined in the song with clapping, breaking into wild applause when she finished the last phrase of her song: *"Jesus is my Lord."* Stepping up to the pulpit, the pastor of the congregation then began to expound the Word of God.*

Spiritual music? Carnal music? How can we discern? Two ways—by "listening" with our *bodies*, as well as with our ears.

First, we need to "zero in" and be sensitive to how different types of music affect our bodies, because there are certain styles of music that contain various rhythms and techniques that are "sensual." Can we honestly believe that God is honored when some of our Christian music is sensual?

As we listen to music, we should evaluate our body's response, since this is key to discerning if the music is carnal or non-carnal.

Second, we can also learn about certain *techniques* used in music which cause these different responses, making the music either truly uplifting (spiritual/non-carnal) or carnal (sensual).

Unavoidably, this somewhat technical "pill" we must digest is the beginning of our development of discernment in the area of music. It's the beginning of our efforts to be diligent to guard our souls so that we may remain *true* to our Living, Almighty, Holy God.

Rest assured that it's not necessary to understand every concept within this chapter. We *do* need to understand, however, that there *are* elements within music that can be dissected and evaluated, elements which make music either non-carnal or carnal. By the final chapter of this book, *everyone* should have the fundamental tools for discerning all music, our ultimate authority being God Himself.

There are five basic elements of music: tone, rhythm, melody, harmony, and tone color.[1] But for the purposes of our study, we'll look at only two, those two being the primary areas around which the controversy regarding "good" and "bad" music seem to revolve. These are *rhythm* and *harmony*.

Rhythm is simply the way notes are arranged in time. Whenever an instrument plays a piece of music, it plays a rhythm of some sort. The rhythm moves the music along. Some notes are of longer duration than others, so to unify a piece of music, we count rhythm patterns in units called *beats*. Each group of beats makes up what's called a *measure*. We start over at the number one after the designated beats in a measure have been counted. This is what makes four/four time, three/four time, two/four time, and so on. The first number indicates how many beats we'll count in a measure before we start the counting over again.

Added to these arrangements of notes is an important element of rhythm called *accent*. Accent means that certain notes are to be played a little stronger than the others so that (1) by regular, predictable placement the music sounds organized; and (2) interest is added to the piece of music.

Natural and Unnatural (Carnal) Rhythms[†]

A simple melody or piece of music that sounds "organized," balanced, and clean, we'll call a *natural* rhythm.

Think of a waltz. The accents are placed on the first beat (or note) of every measure. In other words, we hear: ONE two three; ONE two three; ONE two three, as in the song "Edelweiss" in the movie *The Sound of Music*. A march also has accents on the first beat of every measure: ONE two; ONE two; ONE two, as in John Philip Sousa's "Stars and Stripes Forever."

These are examples of natural rhythms, because the strongest accents are placed on the first note of each measure, setting an orderly, predictable pattern. Even in an orchestra where many instruments play different rhythms,

41

we hear a *unified*, organized effort to follow this rule of accenting the first beat of every measure.

So, in good music, natural rhythms *support* the melody of the music, and, in fact, basically *are* the melody. The rhythm doesn't fight against the melody, neither does it stand out. Essentially, a natural rhythm is a straightforward, clean-sounding melody, with or without complementary harmonization or orchestration.

In contrast, any rhythm that appears unrelated to the melody—by repetition and/or dominance—we'll call an *unnatural* rhythm. A rhythm that is unrelated to the melody is the first and most obvious type of unnatural rhythm because it is the noticeable "beat." To demonstrate this, let's take the melody to Martin Luther's "A Mighty Fortress Is Our God," which is counted in four/four time.[†]

The first beat of each measure is accented: (four); ONE two THREE four; ONE two THREE four; ONE two THREE four; ONE two THREE (four). This translates as: a; MIGHT-y FOR-tress; IS our GOD a; BUL-wark NEV-er; FA-il-ING our...By itself, this is an organized, *natural* rhythm.

Now imagine an *additional* rhythm (usually played by a percussion instrument or bass guitar), but this time the accents are placed on the second and fourth beats (called the *offbeat*): one TWO three FOUR; one TWO three FOUR. If this rhythm and the previous one were put together, would the music still be orderly? On the contrary, the second rhythm is *unnatural* because it *does not support the melody and, in fact, is an entity in itself.* (Further illustrations can be heard via a rock music radio station. Identify a song's melody, then identify the *additional* beat.)

This accented second-and fourth-beat rhythm pattern (accented offbeat) is the most typical example of an unnatural rhythm. Sometimes unnatural rhythms are more complex: one and TWO and three and FOUR and; one and TWO and three and FOUR and. A bass instrument might play a repetitious rhythm, such as, one TWO three FOUR AND; one TWO three FOUR; one—with or without a percussive instrument also accenting the second and fourth beats. Another common rhythm is ONE (two) AND THREE (four); ONE (two) AND THREE (four). (These examples are not set in stone. Unnatural rhythms are many and varied. The illustrations I've given are only a starting point for learning how to identify such rhythms.)

Unnatural rhythms like these have been heard by every one of us while driving, especially when stopped at a stoplight. Haven't we all heard those deep, repetitious rhythms reverberating from a nearby car? We can't hear a melody— just those rhythms. Turning the volume down doesn't make them go away. They are still there, conflicting with the melody of the music.

Common to most of these "beat" unnatural rhythms is the fact that they are *sensual, repetitious,* and *identifiable* (can be easily heard *in addition to* the melody). Sometimes these rhythms are *driving* (loud and obtrusive); sometimes they're *subtle.* Most of the time they're played by a drum or bass guitar—and totally disregard support of the melody. Moreover, many times when we hear the offbeats "two" and "four" accented (or any other unnatural beat, for that matter), they appear to be "just there," for no apparent reason other than to clutter the music. A "gratuitous" beat, so to speak.

Most music that contains these types of unnatural rhythms begins by establishing the beat (really the unnatural rhythm) which we hear *before* the melody is added.

Sometimes the opposite is true—first an introduction of the melody is heard, then the repetitious, unnatural rhythm is added.

A simple test will identify music that does or does not contain these kinds of unnatural rhythms: remove the melody. If a *repetitious* rhythm pattern remains (usually percussion or bass guitar), it's an unnatural rhythm. If no such repetitious rhythm pattern remains, the music is balanced and orderly. There may still be harmony and/or some clean-sounding complementary rhythms, but it will be clear that these support the *same* accented first note of each measure, as well as enhance the basic rhythm of the melody.

Another element of rhythm is called *syncopation*. Syncopation in music occurs when accents are placed on beats that are *not normally* accented;[2] this enlivens the music. But syncopation must not be confused with repetitious, accented (percussive) offbeats. True syncopation will *also* support the melody of the music and be a clean, crisp, straightforward rhythm—even if it's percussive.

Ragtime music is a good example of the use of syncopation, as well as folk-dancing music from traditional ethnic cultures, such as Spain's *flamenco*, the *polka* of Germany, and the Polish *mazurka*. Sometimes these use a clean, crisp, quick, and snappy rhythm on the off-beat that actually enhances the melody, because the first beat of each measure is still leading the melody's rhythm pattern. Toe-tapping or clapping to every beat of the music is a common response, and one can almost imagine the folk dancing of days gone by. This is unlike the unnatural rhythm patterns played *in addition to* a melody and which evoke a sensual hip-swaying or body-jerking response.

Syncopation can *also* be considered an unnatural rhythm at times. It's the *delivery* of the syncopation that distinguishes it as natural or unnatural. Syncopation done correctly creates a clean-sounding, straightforward rhythm which enhances the music.

When syncopation is used incorrectly, the sound is not quite so clean and straightforward. Instead, it sounds jazzy. Boogie-woogie music is a clear example of unnatural syncopation.

Similarly, some *melody* rhythms—like unnatural syncopation—can qualify as unnatural rhythms because they "tease" the listener by holding certain notes just a little longer than "straight" counting. This is true of blues, swing, and jazz music. (The "Pink Panther" theme comes to mind.) Just remember that a melody with natural rhythms should be straightforward and clean sounding.

In general, the most important thing to remember about all rhythms is this: If it supports the melody, if the melody and possible complementary instrumentation moves the music along (including straightforward, crisp syncopation), and if the strongest accent is on the first beat of each measure, it's a natural and balanced rhythm. If there's an *additional*, *repetitious* rhythm pattern that stands out from the melody and *competes* with it, it's an unnatural and out-of-balance rhythm, no matter how quiet or obtrusive it is. (Traditional marches are included in the category of *natural* rhythms because their percussion rhythms are played "straight" and "crisp." They support the first beat of each measure and, usually, the melody's rhythm.)

Additionally, any time a rhythm, melody, or syncopation is delivered in a way that makes the torso want to react independantly, these, too, are sensual, unnatural rhythms.

The natural rhythms of "pure" music suggest orderliness and balance. Unnatural rhythms suggest unbalance, chaos, and sensuality. The principles in Scripture teach us that God is a God of order and holiness; therefore, the music we listen to should also follow the principles of order and purity.

Harmony (in the music of our Western civilization) is based on the idea of notes sounded together, as in a chord, and has two opposite components: *consonance* and *dissonance*. When a chord sounds smooth and pleasant, we say it's consonant. If the chord sounds rough and tense, it's dissonant. Additionally, dissonance can be heard by means of an instrument such as an electric guitar, which sometimes leaves the listener feeling as if he's just heard fingernails scraped across a chalkboard. That's certainly not a soothing sound.

The dictionary defines dissonance as:

> 1. Discord. 2. A combination of tones that sounds harsh and is often suggestive of an unrelieved tension.[3]

Doesn't this "unrelieved," or unresolved, tension in the music give us a picture of what Paul wrote about in the book of Romans—the struggle between our flesh and our spirit?[4]

Unrelieved tension can also be caused by those unnatural rhythms that conflict with the melody, because two very different things are going on at the same time: an orderly melody and an unnatural, repetitious (percussive) rhythm. Furthermore, the melody will have a sense of beginning, middle, and ending, whereas an unnatural, repetitious rhythm is *never* resolved. Added to these, all unnatural rhythms are *sensual*, and each one of these techniques works to create unrelieved tensions.

These unrelieved tensions are not only a "picture" of the Christian's struggle between the flesh and the spirit, they actually *contribute to that struggle,* because the sensual sounds they create appeal to our lower, fleshly (sensual) self. The Bible calls this fleshly self "carnal"—our old sin nature.[5]

Returning to our example of the vibrating rhythms experienced in the car…we've all "felt" those rhythms in our bodies. The high volume simply intensifies our observance of the rhythm's effect on us. Unnatural rhythms played over and over become more appealing to us because we can "experience" the music with our bodies.[6] It's not the melody or the lyrics we are responding to; it's the additional, repetitious rhythms. We may protest that we're being ministered to by the lyrics, and in some cases this may be true. But we're *also* being affected by the carnal rhythms. Because we've been desensitized, we're unaware of the effect on our body when such rhythms are played at a lower volume or when they appear to be integrated with the melody. But when unnatural rhythms are played by percussion or deep-toned instruments such as the bass guitar, and the melody is removed, we see (or feel) that such rhythms are indeed appealing to our flesh. We'll either feel uncomfortable or our bodies will want to move to the *unnatural* beat.

It's difficult to convey these rhythms and sounds on paper, but I think most of us know in our hearts what we're discussing here. Some music is simply carnal and some music is not. But God is *not* a God of carnality or sensuality. He has placed in Christians a yearning to gain victory over improper fleshly desires. Unfortunately, unnatural rhythms and sensual sounds encourage us to fulfill fleshly desires; they do not help us gain victory. Should, then, our Christian music contain such devices?

In short, good music—music which doesn't appeal to our flesh—should contain the following elements:
• A melody that moves along with relatively straightforward rhythms (no "teasing").
• An orderliness to the melody and overall musical piece, established by accents on the first note (beat) of every measure.
• Possible complementary orchestrational rhythms (of various instruments) that support the first beat of every measure (*and* the melody) and are unobtrusive and "clean."
• Chords that sound smooth and pure. No dissonances.
• An obvious *lack* of an additional, identifiable, repetitious, sensual rhythm (usually with some offbeat accents), played by a bass guitar or percussion instrument, which is unrelated to the melody.
• Does *not* encourage the body (torso) to respond with improper movements.

Discernment of music doesn't have to be as complicated as all of this may appear. It's sufficient to know that there *are* elements in music which, when arranged and played in certain ways, create sounds that appeal to the flesh. *Every* Christian has the ability to discern all music through the Holy Spirit Who indwells him. We simply must be willing to submit to His will in the area of music, as in all other areas in our life.[§]

Chapter Five Notes

[*] Based on an actual event with some change in detail to protect those involved.
[†] The term *natural* is used to identify musical rhythms that are *noncarnal*. *Unnatural* rhythms are rhythms that make music *carnal*, and

because such music encourages sensual feelings and/or body movements, these rhythms should be "unnatural" to the Christian's lifestyle.
‡ Third beats in four/four time also get a *slight* accent, but the first beat—the *downbeat*—is always accented the strongest.
§ I realize I'm defining "good" music in terms of what we know in Western civilization. However, *any* culture can have "carnal" music and "non-carnal" music, and it's up to the Christians in those cultures to seek out what is "good and true and pure."[7] All of us are accountable and should offer only our best to God.

(Although this book deals primarily with the actual music that's *played*, it's important to note here that a vocalist can also use his or her voice to create sensual sounds. Breathiness or a sort of gravelly sound are sometimes employed, as is the practice of "sliding" from one note to another. Jazz musicians also make use of sliding. It's a very sensual technique. Additional "sensual" elements are listed in Appendix Three.)

CHAPTER SIX

A BRIEF HISTORY OF CHRISTIAN MUSIC

*"If the foundations be destroyed, what can the right-
eous do?"*

Psalm 11:3

Our journey through the history of Western-culture music can be pictured as a roller-coaster ride. During the
first nine hundred years of its development (after Christ's
death and resurrection), our roller coaster chugs slowly to
the top of the first hill. As it reaches and crests the top, we
pass between the years 1000 and 1400. The beginning of
our ride down symbolizes the beginning of the Renaissance.
As our ride gathers speed and vitality, so does the development of music throughout the years. And just as we have

mixed emotions about our ride, so there have been mixed emotions about music and its changes through the centuries. Has it become a runaway train?

The development of Christian music as we know it is directly linked to the development of Western-culture music, because the actual history of Western civilization's music "properly begins with the music of the Christian Church."[1]

We don't know much about music in the first years of the Church because there wasn't a reliable method for preserving it in a written form. We do know that the early Christians patterned their worship services after the Jewish synagogue services. Similar to today's worship services, they included readings, the singing of psalms and hymns, prayers, and offerings.[2] The musical style of this time was called *plainsong*, meaning a melody sung without accompaniment,[3] which was unlike the secular music of that period.

Most importantly, the early Christians were careful to reject music connected with festivals, competitions, and dramas of their day, because they wanted to help the new converts wean themselves from their pagan past.[4]

From A.D. 200 to 900 Western music remained primarily religious, with a few developments, notably Gregorian Chant, which was a systematic arrangement of all the musical (plainsong) modes of the Western Church. Entire Psalm texts or selected verses made up three-fourths of the chants, and the chants "were the source and inspiration of a large proportion of all sacred Western music up to the sixteenth century."[5]

It's interesting that even though music during this time was simplistic by our standards, the church men of the early

Middle Ages didn't listen to music to enjoy its aesthetic qualities. They maintained that...

"...Beautiful things exist to remind us of divine and perfect beauty and therefore those seeming beauties of the world which inspire only self-centered enjoyment, or desire of possession, are to be rejected."[6]

To them, music was "...to be judged by its power to uplift the soul to contemplation of divine things."[7] Even so, Augustine, one of the great early Church leaders of this time, struggled with being more moved by the beauty of the singing than by the words being sung![8]

The period between A.D. 900 and 1200 produced more building blocks in the development of music, namely, *polyphony* (two or more melodies sung together). Yet they continued to avoid the use of half-tones (chromaticism) and "...other devices of merely sensuous appeal."[9]

The fourteenth century is significant in that the emphasis in music changed from sacred to secular. New musical styles were devised, rhythms became more diverse and free, and harmonic organization progressed.[10] During this century, the first polyphonic music for an entire Roman Catholic mass was written.[11]

Humanism was born during the Renaissance (1450–1600), the era of "new thinking," and there were two important developments in music. First, simpler rhythms enabled the words to be more readily understandable.[12] (This would help Martin Luther later when he authored new hymns.) Secondly, instrumental music began to accompany or replace vocal parts in polyphonic music,[13] and this ultimately developed into solely instrumental music.[14]

Religious music—particularly the Catholic mass— now (reluctantly) was influenced by secular developments in music.[15]

While Catholic church music continued to evolve from the original plainsong and polyphonic music,[16] the Reformation inspired Martin Luther (1483–1546). Called the "Father of Protestant music in Germany," Luther was also influential upon the civilized world as a whole.[17] His introduction of the chorale (a hymn with four-part harmony) into congregational singing "helped to sow the seeds of a musical renaissance in the German-speaking lands."[18]

As music became more complex and varied through the years that followed (with advancements during the Baroque, Classical, and Romantic Periods), there arose several giants in the realm of composers who were inspired by God. Through them we have wonderful masterpieces such as Handel's *Messiah* and Bach's cantatas. We'll look at a few of those men in the next chapter.

Though it appears that in every age there has been a struggle over what is "worldly" and what is acceptable music for the Church, there have been truly inspired developments along the way. It should also be noted that although the Church resisted change through the centuries then adapted to the musical advancements of the time, we can safely conclude that the music used in the Church up to the mid-twentieth century was never "carnal" in the sense that some music is today. Rhythms were straightforward and supported the melody, and, for the most part, efforts were made to delineate secular and sacred music.

After many of the chorales by Luther, Watts, Wesley, and other noteworthy hymn writers were adopted by most Protestant churches and, more recently, many Catholic churches,[19] congregational church music remained relatively the same until the last half of the twentieth century.[20] Then, as the moral decline of our country increased, so our standard as Christians decreased, and the Church began to reflect this by adopting the world's attitudes toward music—unbiblical attitudes that are demonstrated through sensual, carnal rhythms and musical techniques.

This is unacceptable, because unlike the early Church in the development of religious music, we have the ability to look back through history and observe the many changes music has experienced. Through their struggles we reap the benefits and now have a wealth of music from which to choose.

The unnatural rhythms and sensual sounds contained in much music that has been written during the last half of the twentieth century war with the Spirit as never before. But it's no longer necessary for Christians to adapt to the (carnal) music of our time, because we have before us a vast array of musical styles that *are* uplifting to the soul.

CHAPTER SEVEN

MEN WHO HAVE INFLUENCED WESTERN-CULTURE MUSIC

"For as he thinketh in his heart, so is he…"
Proverbs 23:7

"Around five o'clock… it became very dark. Suddenly, there was a great flash of lightning which illuminated the death chamber, accompanied by violent claps of thunder. At the flash of lightning, Beethoven opened his eyes, raised his tightly clenched right hand, and fell back dead."[1]

Without question, there have been brilliant composers throughout the centuries who have influenced music as we've come to know it. Key to most of the composers' musical genius was their deep, abiding faith in God. As we

57

learn more about these men, it becomes evident that what was in their hearts profoundly affected their music—providing us with a rich musical legacy full of order, vitality, and depth. But not all composers had faith in God and this, too, affected the music they created. Let's look briefly at the lives of some of these gifted musicians.

As mentioned before, Martin Luther (1483–1546) has been called the "Father of Protestant music in Germany."[2] Although some people of his time wanted to suppress hymn singing because it reminded them of the Roman Catholic masses, he would have none of it. "Music," he said, "is a gift from God, not from Man."[3]

One of Luther's fervent desires was that the congregation actively take part in the service. So in 1523 he began the task of writing hymns in the German language that could be set to music. His intentions were:

> "…To follow the example of the prophets and the ancient Fathers of the Church, and to make a collection of a certain number of psalms for the people, so that the Word of God may be kept alive in their hearts by song."[4]

In 1524 a collection of religious songs was published by Johann Walther, under Luther's direction. Luther states in the preface of this collection, "…I should like young people…to have at their disposal something which will rid their minds of lascivious and sensual songs, and teach them instead something wholesome."[5]

John Calvin (1509–1564) was more conservative in his thoughts about music, and texts not found in the Bible were forbidden to be sung. In fact, elaborate music was frowned upon[6] and he stated, "Care must always be taken lest the ear be more attentive to the harmony of the song, than is the mind to the spiritual meaning of the words."[7]

The seventeenth century brings us the music of well-known composers such as Vivaldi, Bach, and Handel.

Antonio Vivaldi (ca.1678–1741), known mainly for his music for stringed instruments, was trained for the priesthood, as well as in music. He became head of the Conservatory of the Ospedale della Pieta. There he wrote more than four hundred concertos for their musical programs, and it's there that he "often recited psalms and prayed out loud while walking in the corridors of the Pieta."[8]

Johann Sebastian Bach (1685–1750) was born in the same city in which Luther translated the Bible into German, only 150 years later. Throughout Bach's life, the Lutheran hymnbook was a source for his inspiration and musical genius. It's notable that Bach's understanding of the Scriptures, which translated into his music, "has had an enduring influence in music history in terms of health, strength, and order."[9] Many composers who followed Bach confirmed their gratefulness for this influence his music had upon their lives. A devout Christian, on many of his compositions he wrote, "With the help of Jesus," or "To God alone be the glory."[10]

George Frideric Handel (1685–1759) is probably best known for his *Messiah*. Like many other composers of magnificent intellect, his personality was mercurial, and this affected his music in the most profound way. His biblical oratorios were performed in the theaters, which was revolutionary yet misunderstood by both church people and Handel's opposers. Nevertheless, he persevered, and while in the midst of composing the "Hallelujah Chorus" he exclaimed to his servant, "I did think I did see all heaven before me, and the great God Himself!"[11]

As we move into the eighteenth century (called the Age of Reason), we begin to see man's spiritual focus slowly erode.

Franz Joseph Haydn (1732–1809) was in his twenties when the people of his time began to enthusiastically embrace Jean-Jacques Rousseau's *Discourse on the Origin of Inequality* (which stressed freedom from ancient habits and laws). To his credit, Haydn was not among them. He was probably one of the most contented, sane, and productive composers in history. Inspired by Handel's *Messiah*, he composed *The Creation*, an oratorio which he stated was his favorite, "Because in *The Creation*, angels speak, and their talk is of God."[12]

Wolfgang Amadeus Mozart (1756–1791), though twenty-four years younger than Haydn, formed a great friendship with "Papa Haydn," as he called him. Unfortunately, Haydn's Christian influence was not of great consequence, for towards the end of his short life, Mozart turned to Freemasonry* in place of a formal religion. We'll never know for certain whether Mozart wrote his last composition, *Requiem*, to the Lord Jesus Christ or to the pantheistic god that the Masons' written doctrine affirms. But earlier in his life he composed "Alleluia" and "Psalm 117," so it's arguable that at some point his brilliance was directed toward God.[13]

Ludwig van Beethoven (1770–1827) wrote music full of fierce contrast, which he believed expressed both the turmoil and the peace within man. Though a Catholic, he was influenced greatly by the humanistic philosophy of his day and never attended church. "The fact that Beethoven held a world view that excluded spiritual wholeness caused his music to move in a direction of disintegration toward the end of his life."[14]

The nineteenth century was called "Romantic," and indeed the music of this era reflects that with its fluid beauty and, at times, melancholy, as expressed in the works of Chopin, Brahms, Debussy, Liszt, and Tchaikovsky.

Franz Liszt (1811–1886) was a master at the keyboard who had an intense and vibrant personality and a flair for showmanship. Composers that shaped his own music were Paganini, Chopin, and Berlioz. Although he assured his mother in a letter that he believed in eternal salvation and later studied a little for the priesthood, his life was torn between the pleasures of the world and the yearning for spiritual things. Most of us know him best for his piano piece "Liebestraum," which means "Dream of Love."[15]

Johannes Brahms (1833–1897) had a more compassionate and thoughtful soul than did many other composers. His compositions followed the classical traditions of Bach, Handel, Haydn, and Beethoven, and he wrote music that was at once expressive yet "structurally rooted in the past."[16]

In later years Brahms highly regarded Luther's translation of the Bible and said, "In my study I can lay my hand on my Bible even in the dark."[17]

Finally, the twentieth century dawns and with it the advent of Atonality or, simply, music "lacking a traditional key or tonality."[18] The last of the masters include Bartók, Stravinsky, and Prokofiev.

Béla Bartók (1881–1945) integrated folk music into twentieth century music, which typified his style of composing. Described as "dissonant with little melody," his music indicates a spiritual void, and it's no wonder: He avowed that he was an atheist early in his lonely life.[19]

Igor Stravinsky (1882–1971) led the Anti-romantic movement, and common to his work was the unusual. He seemed to be always exploring new sounds, often combining earlier forms of traditional music with more "modern" sounds and rhythms. This was evidenced in the first modern ballet, *The Rite of Spring*, (1913), which dismayed his listeners to the point of riot.[20]

Although a deeply religious man whose day started with prayer, no doubt he was influenced by the diverse cultures he experienced while living on three different continents during his long and varied life. He himself recognized, "The music of the nineteenth and twentieth centuries—it is all secular…'left to our own devices,' we are poor by many musical forms."[21]

The ballets *Cinderella* and *Romeo and Juliet* and the music composed for *Peter and the Wolf* belong to Sergei Prokofiev (1891–1953), who followed the theory, "Pure art for art's sake."[22] His style was called "mechanistic," adventurous, radical. After having the opportunity to work and travel outside his beloved Russia, his talent was later exploited, then destroyed, by the godless Communist system under which he lived.[23]

It's difficult to leave out other significant composers, but these examples show how faith in God, or lack of it, affected each one's music. While some of the great composers of history may not have acknowledged God, we must remember that the foundations they drew from for their own creativity *were* Spiritually inspired, Christ-centered music. The fact that these composers learned from and were influenced by those who had gone before them is important.

It is clear that writers of contemporary Christian music today are also influenced by those who have gone before them. However, why are they letting the *godless* musicians influence their work, when they have at their disposal a repertoire of brilliant, Providentially inspired composers and the Almighty God to guide them?

From the book, *The Gift of Music*, I'd like to share this thought: "Enjoy and appreciate that which is good, but hold in mind that it is with composers as it is with all of us: what we believe affects our total life."[24]

And, I might add, those who come after us.

Chapter Seven Notes

* Many Masons today and throughout history (including many Presidents of the U.S.) have been, and are, devoted Christian men. However, a thorough study of the actual Masonic doctrine—the full teaching of which many Masons are unaware—embraces a concept of God that is contrary to Scripture.

CHAPTER EIGHT

A WORD ABOUT "POP" MUSIC

"…Denying ungodliness and worldly lusts, we should live soberly, righteously, and godly, in this present world."

Titus 2:12

Most people think of popular music as modern-day music, especially music written in the last few decades. That's certainly true, but its history can be traced back to Ancient Greece and Rome. Its many styles include, but are not limited to, country, motion picture music, jazz, rock, and soul. Some well-known classical works (such as the *William Tell Overture*) also may be considered popular music.[1]

The history of a nation can be told in its popular songs. For example, out of the Civil War came "Battle Hymn of the Republic" and "Dixie," while World War I brought us "Over There."[2]

Just because a piece of music is labeled "pop" or, more correctly, "popular," does not necessarily make it "bad music." *There can be dissonance and unnatural rhythms in classical music, and there can be consonance and natural rhythms in popular music.* Applying what we've learned about these elements will enable us to discern for ourselves, with God's help, what is good music. *"But if any of you lacks wisdom, let him ask of God, who gives to all men generously and without reproach, and it will be given to him"* (James 1:5, NASB).

Should we listen only to Christian music? I can't answer for everyone. Each person must *"work out* [his] *own salvation with fear and trembling."*[3]

Scripture itself points to types of music used for purposes other than praising God. For example, in the Parable of the Lost Son,[4] music was used for celebrating, as it was also after David killed Goliath.[5] And II Samuel 1:19–27 is David's song of lament over the loss of Saul and Jonathan.

Even though the Bible acknowledges the use of (secular) music in daily life, does that mean that our "everyday" music can be carnal, in the sense of containing unnatural rhythms, dissonances, or other sensual sounds? Ideally, no. Neither should the words contradict Scripture. For *"in all things we are a new creature,"*[6] and we are *"created in Christ Jesus unto good works."*[7]

There *is* a lot of good secular music that doesn't compromise our Christian values. Personally, I think we'd be missing a wealth of music that shares, by its message, the drama and joys of our human experience if we were to limit our listening to strictly Christian music. (Think of the wonderful musicals like *The Sound of Music*; the glorious classics; rousing marches; and even some ethnic folk music.)

However, if all we *do* is listen to music, then we must consider the question, "Has music become an idol?"

A relatively recent development in popular music is New Age music.* To accept New Age music as okay is to be naive. As the end of time draws near, Satan will use every available tool to deceive the people, including imitating the styles of good music.

As never before, we need to be spiritually alert in discerning that which is "good and true and pure."

New Age music is extremely deceptive, and therefore extremely dangerous. It's significant to note that it "is very much an international phenomenon."[18] (A possible implication of this is the unifying of the world's people, through the music, into a One World Religion.) Already, New Age terms such as "stress reduction" and "healing" are appearing in the marketing promotions of some Christian music.

How do we discern this type of music? It's nearly always labeled New Age. And as Christians, we should take care that we don't unknowingly imitate and/or incorporate New Age philosophies or practices in any way, shape, or form—by musical styles or by use of key phrases common to this movement.

New Age music, almost always solely instrumental, basically follows traditional classical music patterns, yet with simple, contemplative melodies, occasionally using *quiet* unnatural rhythms such as those found in "soft" rock or calmer jazz music. One can also sense the subtle (or not so subtle) influence of Eastern mysticism.[19] The melodies, for the most part, lack structure; that is, there's no sense of beginning, middle, or ending, and they're very repetitive. This repetitiveness could almost be likened to the practice of chanting a *mantra* (a monosyllabic word) over and over, which is a technique used in Eastern-style meditation.

Making use of electronic devices, traditional instruments, and sounds from nature, it's usually soothing to listen to on the superficial level. What's troubling, though, is the motivation behind the music. "New Age music is meant to relax the listener"[20] and "is often used as *an aid in meditation*" (emphasis added).[21†]

True New Age music is the "religious" music of those who practice New Age philosophies. Knowing this, should we as Christians listen to or adopt this type of music? Unfortunately, some contemporary Christian praise music is similar in style to New Age music, containing repetitiveness in both melody and lyrics.

It seems that as time on this earth draws to a close, Christians should be progressively less like those around them, because the world is becoming more evil. Yet, it appears that we are growing increasingly more *like* the world. Not in the practices of overt sin, but in the adoption of habits and attitudes of the world system. Could it be that some people are drawn to New Age music because it offers a "difference" from the world that's lacking in much contemporary Christian music? Our music has blended so much with the world's music that one gets the impression that Christianity is no longer able to provide a life-changing "difference" that many people are seeking.

Make no mistake, I'm not advocating the notion that any music composed past a certain time period is "evil." God inspires men and women today as He has throughout the ages. He also is a loving God to give us beautiful music to celebrate life with, as well as bring praises to Him. Yet we have a responsibility to judge each piece of music to see whether or not it stands up to the light of Scriptural principles. The bottom line is this: All music in a Christian's life—secular and sacred—should be evaluated for its content, both musically and its message...and there should be a "difference" in these two areas.

Chapter Eight Notes

* "New Age music" is a broad term used to classify much contemporary, soothing music. For our purposes, I'm referring here only to New Age music that's meant to be used in New Age practices and that follows New Age philosophies.

Without going into great detail, because there are reliable books available on this subject, suffice it to say that New Age leaders "seek to destroy Christianity."[8] The movement is called the "New Age World Religion" and "denies the existence of a personal God," yet "exalts human potential and scientific progress."[9] Its leaders claim they are "forerunners of the New Age Messiah, a great superhuman world teacher and leader who is soon to come" (the Antichrist in Christian terminology).[10]

To the New Ager, "man is neither sinful nor evil," and "did not need a Savior to atone for sin."[11] Along with this belief, they have taken Christian terms such as God, Christ, salvation, and the Second Coming and twisted them to suit their own hidden purposes.[12]

Altering the mind's consciousness through Yoga, meditation, chanting, drugs, and other means is their way to "salvation."[13] Through this "altered consciousness" they obtain what they call "Christ consciousness,"[14] or being "at one" with all things, and therefore their own god. This idea that "all is god"[15] is the essence of New Age Religion.

Their primary goal: "To establish a One World, New Age Religion and a one world political and social order."[16] Texe Marrs, in his book *Dark Secrets of the New Age*, states, ". . . The New Age World Religion fits all the criteria of the Babylonian harlot church of the latter days."[17]

Many Christians are unknowledgeable about the New Age Movement and may unwittingly be swept into some of its beliefs and prac-

tices. Masterminded by Satan, it is exceedingly cunning and deceptive, permeating all areas of our society.

[†] The meditation of one who practices New Age philosophies is at a
variance with the meditation a Christian practices when thinking on
Scripture. The New Ager is taught Eastern meditation, where one *emp-
ties the mind* "with the goal of attaining 'cosmic consciousness,' one-
ness with all things." Biblical meditation's objective is to *fill the mind*
with God's Word.[22]

CHAPTER NINE

EXCUSES, EXCUSES

"The heart is deceitful above all things, and desperately wicked: who can know it?"

Jeremiah 17:9

M an is a reasonable, rational being, *except* when his personal beliefs are challenged. At such times, he becomes irrational because he acts upon his emotions rather than his intellect, or, if a Christian, he sometimes fails to turn to his true Source for wisdom, aided by study of the Scriptures.

Because music appeals to our emotions, we approach the subject of Christian music *through* our emotions—"digging in our heels" when confronted with problems in music that may concern our personal choice. Perhaps we think that because our musical "preference" is being challenged, we *personally* are being challenged. This shouldn't be the case. We need to distance ourselves from our emotions, look at principles of Scripture, identify and acknowledge the elements in music which are carnal (sensual), and put our new-found knowledge into practice by eliminating such music from our lives. We must realize that it is some *music* which contains the troubling elements, not us. And as with *any* offending matter in our lives it should be "plucked out."[1]

This chapter addresses some of the most common, *emotionally charged excuses* given by people concerning contemporary Christian music, along with biblical principles and our responsibility as Christians that can be applied to each one.

1. *We live in the real world and should be "balanced."*

The implication of this excuse is, "Let's be just a little bit like the world so we won't be too different, and then we won't offend anyone." In part, this is true: we shouldn't offend others, especially believers.[2] Still, because we're Christ's, the world will hate us[3] and what we stand for. The Scriptures *never* direct us to achieve a balance with the world by embracing its precepts, principles, or habits.

To say that we should be balanced, according to the world's standards, yet to choose to listen to music that's out of balance according to God's standards, is actually the opposite of what we should be doing. Our music should be balanced and orderly, and our lives should be "out of balance" in the world's way of thinking.

2. *Everyone has his or her own point of view on music.*

Without doubt, God created each person a unique individual, and this makes the world an interesting place. Nevertheless, as with the way of salvation, everyone can't be right. To continue to listen to "Christian" rock/alternative music that's essentially the same as the music we listened to before we came to the Lord isn't *truly* changing our lifestyle in the area of music. The only thing that has been changed is the lyrics, and that's so we can *justify* our continuing to listen to that type of music.

Sometimes we justify that, because the unnatural rhythms are "polished up" and orchestration has been added to make the music sound more "sophisticated," it is acceptable. Although the result may be more grandiose, those underlying, sensual rhythms remain, however subtle they may be.

Yet, if we refuse to acknowledge that certain music contains carnal/sensual devices and we continue to listen to such music (under the guise that, "For *me* it's acceptable and uplifting"), aren't we suggesting that a little sensuality is okay? Aren't we then setting our own standard? Whose standard are we to follow? A standard of our own making, or The Standard set forth in Scripture by Almighty God?

God's will must be discerned in every aspect of our lives, including our music, and we need to ask ourselves, "Does this truly help me to walk in the Spirit,[4] or am I compromising even a little bit?"

3. *The only way to reach this generation for Christ is by using music they'll listen to.*

Attracting people to the Church with "their" music is deceptive. It's also like saying, "Look, we're a lot like you." If the music in the Church sounds like the music the unbelievers listen to at home or on the street, then how can they perceive us—as believers in Christ—as able to offer them something different that will truly meet their spiritual needs?

Recall from chapter six that the very early Christians were careful not to allow any secular-type music into the Church so they could help the new converts wean themselves from their (pagan) past. Should we do less to help our new converts establish a new life in Christ?

To the younger generation, the Church should be like the responsible parent who provides nourishment for growth and withholds those things that are harmful. A child may *want* something, but what he *needs* may be different. Yet, we are particularly guilty of giving the younger generation what they *want* to hear musically, instead of what they *need* to hear. Is this responsible training?

The Church's purpose is not to please the world. Its purpose is to minister to the saints and to provide a sanctuary *from* the world. Not to undermine the value of beautiful and uplifting music in our worship services, let it be said that if people are serious about finding God, *they will come* to our churches and won't need weekly entertainment to draw them.

If the Church feels a need to draw people with "worldly" sounding music, it's because we, as individual Christians, have failed to share with other people how Christ has changed our lives. The early New Testament Church grew because the people were excited about what God had done for them and went and told others. Today, we've become complacent and rely on the Church to provide programs and entertainment to draw people.

Indeed, these things have their place *at times*; however, in the Bible, religious music is always referred to as a way to praise God and instruct believers.[5] It's never referred to as a means of spreading the Gospel. History itself shows us that all of the great revivals were preceded by fervent prayer and God's people getting serious about His holiness. They were not the result of "religious fervor" brought about through music in the Church. Have we forgotten that *it is the Holy Spirit Who draws people to Christ, not "methods" (including the "right" music) devised by man?*

④ *Music is just an external in our lives, and focusing on the externals is legalism.*

Yes, music is an external, but the music we listen to reflects the condition of our spirit. It's a barometer of what we're thinking about, since music provokes thought, and vice versa. Scripture exhorts us to think on that which is "good and true and pure."[6] If we're changed on the inside, shouldn't the evidence also be apparent on the outside?

God's grace is not a license to do as we please. It's merely a freedom in knowing that we don't have to follow a certain set of rules. However, we as Christians are also given a responsibility to live holy lives.[7] With God's grace, and through the power of the Holy Spirit indwelling us, we can strive to be more like Christ every day.

To attempt to please God on our own, without Jesus Christ (following a list of do's and don'ts we make for ourselves and others) *is* legalism. If we are God-controlled through the indwelling Holy Spirit, we have the power to be free from our sin nature and are enabled to do His will, whatever that may be in our lives. This is *not* legalism.[8]

Is it "legalistic" when we exhort others to not look at sensual (immoral) magazines? Is it "legalistic" when we encourage reasonable, modest dress and behavior? And is it "legalistic" to say that reading literature that stirs up sensual desires isn't pleasing to God? On the contrary, all of these are biblical exhortations to live holy and pure lives. Should we have less of a standard for music? We *must* face the fact that some rhythms and musical techniques *are* sensual, and because the Bible is clear about sensuality, carnal rhythms and sensual techniques have no place in the Christian's music. Consequently, abstaining from carnal musical techniques can in no way be construed as legalistic.

We need to be aware that many times, when confronted with an issue that's close to our heart (our "hot button"), the first thing we cry is, "Legalism!" We react, instead of prayerfully considering what's being said. Consider this: Are we hiding behind the term legalism so that we may excuse certain practices we refuse to give up?

The Christian walk includes denying our self (our old sin nature), and to declare something legalistic is sometimes—oftentimes—a means to avoid dealing with an area in our lives that needs to be submitted to God.

> *"Be not deceived; God is not mocked: for whatsoever a man soweth, that shall he also reap. For he that soweth to his flesh shall of the flesh reap corruption; but he that soweth to the Spirit shall of the Spirit reap life everlasting."*
>
> Galatians 6:7–8

5. *God can use the music for His good.*

God can use *anything, anytime, anywhere* He wants, to draw people to Himself. That, however, does not give Christians freedom to violate biblical principles in order to "reach the lost." God works His perfect will *in spite of* man, not *because of* man's efforts. Our mistaken efforts to add good lyrics to a "rock beat" does not make the rock music better. *It makes the Christian's song worse.* "A little leaven leaveneth the whole lump."[9] God warned the Hebrews many times in the Old Testament not to adopt the ways of the heathen. Jeremiah 10:2 says, *"Thus saith the Lord, Learn not the way of the heathen...."* Are Christians exempt from this admonition?

A quick stroll through your local Christian bookstore's music section will demonstrate how the world's attitudes have crept into Christian music. Some album covers truly cannot be distinguished from secular album covers and, in fact, are downright evil. Why is it that music seems to be an area that we place above submission to God? Like it or not, God wants *total* surrender. The evidence of ungodly attitudes on some Christian album covers is indeed proof that we *have* learned "the way of the heathen," and have *not* submitted ourselves unto the Lord God Almighty. Yet we wonder why our lives lack spiritual power and victory. From God's perspective, partial obedience is still *dis*obedience.

6. *But we are sincere when we sing to God with music that has a beat.*

Certainly some people may sing their praises to God with all their heart—to music containing a rock beat. I would attribute this to a new or uninformed Christian, and I have no doubt that many *are* sincere. At this point it would be acceptable because it *is* their best.

With all due respect to many people whom I know have truly pure motives and hearts that seek after God, we must still consider this: Does pureness of heart override our responsibility to examine and evaluate our methods? Is pureness of heart a viable reason to overlook identifiable faults with our music? A *bad* motive can make a good action wrong. A *good* motive does *not* make a bad action right. We've all heard the saying, "We can be truly sincere, but we can be sincerely wrong."

Yes, God looks upon our hearts. If we have not knowledge, but pure hearts, God is honored. But if we have gained knowledge and have chosen not to act upon it, believing "our motives are pure," does this honor God? The Bible never says to *only* have pure motives. We are exhorted to *"grow in grace, and in the knowledge of our Lord and Savior Jesus Christ."*[10] As we grow, we're to become more like Christ:

> *"...As obedient children,* not fashioning yourselves according to the former lusts in your ignorance: *But as he which hath called you is holy, so be ye holy in* all *manner of conversation;* Because it is written, Be ye holy; for I am holy."*
>
> I Peter 1:14–16 (emphasis added)

7. The Christian musical artists are sincere.

Many are honestly sincere (as indicated above), some aren't. The Bible tells us there are impostors in the Church, so it's likely there are musicians who are posing as Christians.[11] It's also a sobering thing to consider that, because many artists consider themselves to be "ministering" with their music, they will be held accountable for the *kind* of music through which they minister. If an artist is *truly* sincere about spreading the Gospel and teaching people about Jesus Christ, he or she needs to give serious thought to how the listener is affected by the music (not just the words). Is it right that contemporary Christian music should (and does) cause the listener to respond in a manner not pleasing to God (that is, through carnal [sensual] movements and/or sensual dancing, disrespect, imitation of the world, and so on)?

To use music in which the underlying rhythms are carnal (sensual) is actually sending a message that, to believe in Christ, a person's musical practices won't really have to change—that *some* sensuality is acceptable. Yet *that* message isn't in compliance with Scripture. (Reread I Peter 1:14–16 on page 78.)

We also have to look beyond the music to the *delivery* of that music. A person may be saying one thing with his mouth (by way of Christian lyrics), yet be saying something totally different through his body language and/or vocal techniques. Not only does sensual music *contribute* to the worldly attitudes and actions that subtly come into the Church through a performer's delivery of a "message" through song, but it also *promotes* self-glorification rather than the exaltation of a Holy God.

So, just as we wouldn't think of seeking out a heretic for a preacher, so we should be careful in our choices of musical artists and the messages they convey—through their music, through their lyrics, and through their delivery of both.

8. *What about "dancing before the Lord"? We can't dance if there's no beat.*

Researched back to the Hebrew and Greek, almost all dancing in Scripture refers to a "round."[12] The dictionary defines a round dance as:

> 1. a dance performed by couples with circular or revolving movements. 2. a folk dance with dancers in a circle.[13]

Most likely the people in Bible times performed folk-type dances.[†]

When David danced before the Lord (see II Samuel 6:12–16), the Hebrew words indicate that he leaped, jumped, and whirled for joy.[14]

What does this have to do with us today, and how does this apply to music? We need to be aware that there are acceptable and unacceptable body/dance movements, and the *type* of music *dictates* our response. In historical "period" movies, we see that when they danced they *moved their bodies (torsos) as a unit*. Music with straightforward rhythms and harmonious melodies was conducive to this. They danced such dances as the minuet, waltz, and folk dance. This is further demonstrated in classical ballet.

Music that contains unnatural rhythms causes the body to move independently in sensual movements, reminiscent of pagan dances. With the advent of rock music, and even before that because of the influences we studied earlier, "Young people...adopted the form and gestures of African dances that suited the music."[15]

We've all seen "sensual" dancing. Essentially, sensual dancing requires sensual music. This type of dancing is an outward manifestation of the inward effect of the carnal music. And although as Christians we (hopefully) wouldn't participate in such a blatant display of disobedience, much contemporary Christian music contains rhythms and/or other techniques that cause our bodies to respond in a sensual manner, yet to a lesser degree.

In these last days our knowledge of this world may have increased, but our perception of God as a *Holy* God has decreased, and we've become "desensitized" in the area of dancing, as well.

9. *I listen to contemporary Christian music, and I can't hear anything wrong.*

God gave us five senses through which to experience life—taste, touch, sight, hearing, and smell—and these are wonderful when used as He intended. The problem develops when outside stimuli are rebelliously perverted in such a way that sensual responses are elicited that cannot be fulfilled in a righteous manner. Likewise, music that has been corrupted so that it appeals to our carnal senses instead of our spirits creates in us a desire to hear *more* carnal music so that we may "satisfy" our flesh. At this point, the addition of Christian lyrics creates confusion. We *know* we should be worshipping and praising the Lord, so we justify that the words "make it all right." However, the Bible speaks about the flesh and the (Holy) Spirit being at odds.[16] Therefore, "carnal" Christian music is unacceptable.

The reason this is not so clear to some is that their spiritual awareness of the sensuality in the music has been deadened in this area, simply by having experienced the stimuli (carnal rhythms, etc.) so often that they are no longer aware of how wrong the sensual response is. *If we see, do, or hear something long enough, it becomes acceptable and no longer affects the conscience.*

Just because a person can't "hear" or discern the sensuality of certain music *doesn't* mean there are no sensual rhythms or other sensual devices in the music. Many people haven't experienced the leading of the Holy Spirit, but does that mean He does not exist? And if we've become so desensitized that we cannot discern, are we excused from evaluating our music? Won't each and every one of us one day give an account for how we have conducted our lives?[17]

Additionally, we are told to "keep our hearts,"[18] which means to *guard* our hearts from those things that can hinder our walk with the Lord. Music is an important aspect of our lives, and because it directly affects our emotions it's extremely important that it pass the scrutiny of biblical principles—both in the lyrics and in the music itself.

Therefore, the excuse that we "can't hear anything wrong" isn't a valid argument until we're willing to look at our music through the magnifying glass of God's Word and His principles.

10. *Our church services will be "dead" without upbeat music.*

First of all, no one said church music had to be dull and lifeless to be spiritual. But on the other hand, we shouldn't judge a church's spirituality by its music. To judge a church solely by its music is to *"heap up for… [ourselves] teachers, having itching ears."*[19] We shouldn't equate a church's being "alive" with exciting music that "tickles" our ears and entertains us. It's not *our* efforts that make a church alive. It's the presence of the Holy Spirit.

Do we "sing because we're happy,"[20] or are we happy because we sing? This is an important distinction to make. If a church is full of Spirit-filled, Christ-centered Christians, the music will have life and meaning because these people are singing to the Lord from their hearts. But to put on a show with upbeat, entertaining music in order to get people "revved up" is a mistake, because this promotes false feelings of spirituality that last only for a brief time and are not life-changing.

Truly, the right music can enhance the worship service and aid in our personal path to worship. But it shouldn't be the focus. Remember the purpose of worship: To ascribe worth to a Holy God; to give Him *reverence*. It's not to please ourselves, although our personal edification and satisfaction *will* be a result of true worship.

11. *We need a Christian "counterculture" in music.*

There are many developments in human history that benefit all mankind—saved or unsaved. Many of these were invented by unsaved people. That, in and of itself, isn't bad, because many inventions are for the good of all (for example: automobiles, telephones, medicines, and computers). However, when any advancement or invention grows distorted so that it causes harm or impedes spiritual growth, it becomes wrong for the Christian. From its inception, rock music is such a distortion and a compromise of our spiritual values.

We're told in II Timothy 2:22 to *"flee from youthful lusts"* (NASB), and I Peter 2:11 tells us to *"abstain from fleshly lusts, which war against the soul."* Because of its carnal nature, rock music of any sort (including Christian rock and its many derivatives, however subtle) works contrary to these exhortations.

Scripture is also very clear in its instruction to not offend or cause another believer to stumble. Yet it's disturbing that Christian rock music has violated this principle.[21] Because of this type of music's wide scope of influence and exposure—through albums, concerts, and radio—the potential for further offense is broad. It's not enough, nor is it responsible "Christianship"[‡] to simply tell someone not to listen. The truly meek and humble will put others first.

No, a counterculture isn't the answer. Perhaps instead of imitating what's wrong in music, we should be setting a new standard, with orderly and Godly music that far surpasses what's offered in the secular world. After all, isn't that what Bach, Handel, and other great masters did who served the same God we serve?

12. *You can't prove to me a certain beat or rhythm is wrong.*

In light of all we have learned to this point—how unnatural rhythms suggest a lack of order (God is a God of order); their lack of straightforwardness (implying deceptiveness, but God is never deceptive); the conflict between the rhythm of the melody and an additional, repetitious rhythm (which parallels the Christian's conflict between his renewed spirit and his old sin nature); unnatural rhythms' origination from pagans who sought to please their flesh (God says not to learn their ways); the rebellion which was the catalyst of rock music (Christians should not imitate rebellious music); and most importantly, Scripture's direction in Ephesians 5:19 and Colossians 3:16 to sing "spiritual songs" (meaning non-carnal, that is, music which reflects our new, regenerated life in Christ and does not appeal in any way to our old, unregenerate, carnal way of life)—I can say that the balance of proof against unnatural rhythms weighs heavily on the side of being inappropriate for Christian music. Is there such evidence to tip the scales and prove that unnatural rhythms *are* acceptable? And which side of the scales will pass the test of comparison to principles of Scripture—principles which *are* clear and unambiguous?

13. *Martin Luther set his hymns to the tunes (worldly songs) of his day.*

This is a lame excuse, and a half-truth at best. Although Martin Luther (and other hymn writers who followed him) may have borrowed from "popular" folk tunes, or even tavern music, the music itself didn't stay in its original form.[8] The simple melodies they used were *rewritten into chorale form* which best suited the new lyrics intended for congregational singing.[23]

Luther's practice of adapting basic tunes to chorale form is vastly different from today's practice of simply putting Christian lyrics to secular-type music. Attempting to redeem unacceptable music by *only* adding Christian lyrics is the same as adding oil to water. *"What fellowship hath righteousness with unrighteousness? and what communion hath light with darkness?"*[24] As Luther (and other hymn writers) demonstrated, *both* the music and the lyrics must be made suitable for Christian hymns and songs.

In chapter seven, "Men Who Have Influenced Western-Culture Music," we saw that a composer's heart-condition affected his music—much of which contained *no lyr-ics*. So it's clear that music itself *can* be evaluated. Simply adding the "right" words doesn't transform the whole piece. If the music itself is sick, adding Christian lyrics is like putting a Band-Aid on a disease that requires major surgery.

We can also observe that circumstances were different in Luther's day: "Transference of melodies was already fairly frequent at that time," and, "In the religious and secular compositions of this period and the preceding one, there are a number of melodic motives** which often recur, each time with different words."[26] (In other words, composers borrowed from each other.)

Additionally, it wasn't until after the turn of the century (1600) that congregational singing (in German-Protestant churches) was accompanied by organ. Up till then, congregational singing was most likely unaccompanied;[27] however, *alternate* verses may have been played by the organist.[28] "But Luther was not in favour of organ-playing during the service; he seldom mentions it in any of his writings."[29]

This indicates a far different state of affairs than what exists today in Christian music, especially when we consider the many instruments that now accompany secular and religious music and that create complex and varied sounds foreign to Luther's day.

The practice of pointing to another Christian so that we may excuse our own behavior is not to be commended. Only God knows the other person's true motivations and circumstances. As for Luther, his musical endeavors—which have been offensive to very few people, if any—have borne much fruit and withstood the test of time, and they will continue to do so.

Martin Luther's work came at a time in history (the Reformation) when new innovations in church music were deemed necessary, and he himself "felt that he was inaugurating a new period of song."[30] There has not been such a time since; therefore, to compare our imitation of ungodly music with the works of such a distinguished and Godly man as Martin Luther is like comparing apples and oranges. *There is no comparison.*

14. *We should be more concerned that the music draws us closer to God, rather than if the music is carnal.*

Unquestionably, our hearts desire should be to draw closer to God. However is *our* experience the primary focus, or is worshipping God the primary focus? It is God whom we worship, and therefore it should be God whom we please. Which would be more pleasing to God—carnal Christian music or non-carnal Christian music? Carnal Christian music is not the only means of drawing closer to Him. I Samuel 15:22 states, *"To obey is better than sacrifice...."* Obedience always results in drawing closer to God, so instead of asking, "Does the (carnal) music draw me closer to God?" we should be asking, "Am I pleasing God by *obeying* His word in the area of music?"

15. *If "carnal" Christian music is wrong, then why is it so successful?*

Christians yearn for a deeper relationship with Christ. We want to *experience* Him. This "yearning" is artificially "satisfied" through carnal music because, as discussed in chapter five, we can " experience" the music with our bodies. However, this "satisfaction" is short-lived, resulting in a constant need for further exposure to carnal music in order to remain "satisfied." Because we are carnally satisfied, we are hindered from experiencing a deeper walk with the Lord.

Carnal Christian music is successful because, just like secular rock music, it satisfies our carnal nature—our "flesh." It's an instant gratification that doesn't require active participation in prayer and Bible study.

Just because something is successful doesn't necessarily mean God's "stamp of approval" is on it. Do we attribute the success of secular rock music to God? To have the approbation of many people is not the true measure of success. Jesus' message was not always a "popular" message.[31] One day, each and every one of us will be judged,[32] and our "success" on earth will be measured by how we obeyed and served God, not how we pleased men.

16. *The Bible doesn't give any direct command or teaching about the type of music we should use.*

This, of all the excuses, is where most Christians "hang their hats" in *defense* of their musical practices. But it's no longer valid because we've shown that Ephesians 5:19 and Colossians 3:16 *do* give us direction. Even if those Scriptures weren't there, biblical principles *still* apply. Just as there are *other* issues the Bible doesn't directly address, Christians *have* been able to glean principles and truths: gambling; the concept of the Trinity; the principle of modest behavior; the principle of sowing and reaping; and so on. The Proverbs alone are full of principles that can be applied to various aspects of our lives. If *any* issue is unclear to us, does that lessen our responsibility before a Holy God?

There's a certain religious group that claims that because there is no direct teaching about the Trinity, it doesn't exist. But because diligent scholars have sought the truth—gleaning and searching the Scriptures—born-again believers accept the concept of the Trinity.

In chapter eleven we'll see how biblical principles can be followed through a line of reasoning and then applied—in this case to the area of music.

These are some difficult issues concerning contemporary Christian music and, when discussed, are enough to raise anyone's dander. But most of these excuses boil down to the following questions *each one of us* must answer for himself before a Holy God: Are pure motives enough *in God's eyes* to overlook the carnal rhythms and sensual techniques used in some Christian music, whether or not we think those techniques affect us personally? Would God ever ask us to violate scriptural principles in order to minister to others?

Chapter Nine Notes

* The New American Standard Bible says, "…in all your behavior."

† Folk dancing is still practiced in some Hebrew worship services.

‡ *Christianship*: the manner in which we conduct our Christian life, that is, responsibly or irresponsibly.

§ In actuality, *Luther's* practice was to adapt mostly religious folk songs and pre-existing hymns or chants, or use melodies of his own invention.[22]

** A "motive," in this instance, is a series of notes (a musical idea) repeated throughout a piece of music.[25]

CHAPTER TEN

WHAT DIFFERENCE
DOES IT MAKE?

*"But strong meat belongeth to them that are of full age,
even those who by reason of use have their senses exer-
cised to discern both good and evil."*

Hebrews 5:14

NOTE: Some of the ideas within this chapter are rather
strong. It's not my intention to discredit any artist,
performer, or person in his choice of music, nor to
question a person's "spirituality" or love for the Lord
Jesus Christ. It *is* my intention to stretch our thinking concerning music and how we react to it, as well
as expose and challenge sensual music techniques
used in Christian music.

Some things in life are easily discernible as right or wrong. Some things aren't. It then becomes necessary for us to glean and apply scriptural truths in order to arrive at an acceptable conclusion.

In these latter days we've grown lazy in our pursuit of biblical knowledge and wisdom. We've grown lazy in our prayer life. And as a result of these, we haven't developed the spiritual "muscle" necessary for discerning those things that are neither black nor white.

We live in a world of instant gratification. But wisdom that comes from God is not instant.

Beyond the fact that most people agree that some secular music doesn't edify the believer, probably most people haven't given much thought to contemporary Christian music. Maybe some don't like it, but until now they have not been able to put their finger on the exact reason they don't like it.

And maybe there are some who say, "What difference does it make? I love the Lord, and I know I'm a Christian, so what difference does it make whether or not I listen to contemporary Christian rock music?"

Music is all around us; it's hard to escape. We go to the store—it's there. We eat in a restaurant—it's there. We cheer at our favorite event—it's there. Everywhere we go—it's there.

Because it's everywhere around us, our private lives give us the opportunity to "*come out from among them and be separate*"[1] in the area of music. This provides us with an opportunity to witness. But *how* are we witnessing with our music?

Let's say you're at home, listening to Christian music that is "questionable," music that contains unnatural rhythms. Your neighbor stops by. The first thing he hears (be honest) isn't the words of the music, but the music it-self—those rhythms that he's familiar with in his own life. What does this tell him? That your life isn't much different from his.

Now the scenario changes. This time you're listening to music that has straightforward rhythms that support the melody. Your neighbor stops by; he perceives you as *different*. Why? Ask yourself this: How many people do you know listen only to music that's good, as we've previously defined good music?

In our culture, what we listen to reflects who we are. If we as Christians listen to the same types of music (unnatural rhythms, sensual techniques, and dissonance) as the world, how are we exhibiting the characteristics of a "peculiar people"[2] in our music?

In truth, many of us are afraid of being perceived as different. But God has called us out to *be* different. What kind of music we listen to does make a difference…in *our* lives because the music we listen to should encourage us to be like Christ…in *other* people's lives as they perceive us to be different and, in turn, are drawn to Christ through us.

Likewise, we need to be careful that we don't unknowingly *adjust* our Christianity instead of truly change to be like Christ. The Bible says, *"…If any man be in Christ, he is a new creature: old things are passed away; behold, all things are become new"* (II Corinthians 5:17). Notice it didn't say "old things are *altered* to become more acceptable."

The life of a Christian is indeed a pilgrimage. Let's ask ourselves, "How am I more holy, more like Christ today, than I was yesterday?" If we're serious about our walk with the Lord Jesus Christ, it seems that we would want to hold a magnifying glass to each area of our lives in order to "separate the wheat from the chaff." God in His goodness and mercy won't give us more than we can handle, but He greatly desires that we seek Him in every area of our lives.

Let's not be like Israel, of whom Paul says:

"For I bear them record that they have a zeal of God, but not according to knowledge. For they being ignorant of God's righteousness, and going about to establish their own righteousness, have not submitted themselves unto the righteousness of God."

Romans 10:2–3

Even though Paul is speaking here about salvation (by way of the cross of Jesus Christ), this is also a *principle* that can be applied to all areas of our lives.

The music we listen to in our churches makes a difference also. One of the Church's missions is to admonish (instruct) the believer *"...in psalms and hymns and spiritual songs . . ."* (Colossians 3:16). But when there is carnal music in the Church, the "admonishing" is negated because of the music's appeal to the flesh, which creates an "emotional high."

This emotional high (or energy) that's experienced from carnal music actually inhibits us from seeking the true joy and freedom found in Jesus Christ. It's a cheap substitute for the energy that comes from being free from the power of sin. The energy that comes from being set free from the power of sin is from God.

In fact, accepting this cheap substitute can contribute to the creation of a Laodicean church,[3] because it makes the Church "feel" that it's spiritual, when in truth it is *"...wretched, and miserable, and poor, and blind, and naked."*[4]

In the *same* worship service, one person can claim that the contemporary music helps him to worship and "feel" God's presence, yet another person can be truly *grieved* in his spirit by such music. Something here is definitely wrong. If there's nothing wrong, as many argue, justify, and defend, then *why* is there a controversy? Arguably, those persons who are so disturbed by contemporary Christian (rock) music are actually sensing the caution of the Holy Spirit, yet they don't understand that this caution is in reference to the carnal and/or sensual techniques in the music.

Music can, and does, affect the emotions. Recall how Saul's soul was soothed when David played the harp.[5] If we can be soothed through music, it only stands to reason that we can be "energized" as well. Without realizing it, unaware, well-meaning Christians are turning to their (contemporary Christian) music for the "high" that carnal music can foster *instead* of turning to God for their spiritual filling. If there's any doubt about this fact, eliminate the words, listen only to the music, and evaluate the response. Is there a *pureness* in your soul that accompanies the exhilaration you feel through the music, or does the music, indeed, appeal to your flesh? We must be ever diligent, *"for Satan himself is transformed into an angel of light"* (II Corinthians 11:14).

Satan would have us believe that because a piece of carnal religious music "energizes" us it's acceptable. However, the energy that comes from Godly music, experienced through a *cleanness and pureness* in our souls, cannot be truly imitated by the "father of lies." The enticement of carnal music *is* his lie, and by accepting the enticement because it appeals to our flesh—satisfies our *carnal* self—we are unaware that we have not *truly* worshipped a Holy God.[6]

We automatically assume that, because we "feel" something during the song service, or even during our own private listening, we're feeling the presence of the Holy Spirit. If one were to conduct an experiment and listen to several types of music, all without lyrics (for example, march music, melancholic music, and a quick-stepping waltz), *each* of these would evoke a completely different response. Each would affect our emotions and either energize us or cause us to be reflective, maybe even sad.

So to make a blanket statement such as, "I really feel the Holy Spirit's presence," when we hear certain music is not always a true statement. We should be very careful to identify the true source of our "feeling." The Holy Spirit isn't dependent upon music. Doesn't the Holy Spirit fill us with joy and peace without music? Maybe *we* are the ones dependent upon the music to give us a "feeling" that the Holy Spirit is present.

If our music is truly a form of worship, it will flow through our souls and then our worship will flow up to God—resulting in a pureness in our spirits given by the Holy Spirit. It will be like a complete circle. If the music is carnal, this "flow" will *end* with us because we are, in reality, unknowingly satisfying our *flesh*. Our motives may be right, and the lyrics may give an apparent validity to those motives, but remember, the "flesh" and the (Holy) Spirit are at odds. *"For the flesh sets its desire against the Spirit, and the Spirit against the flesh; for these are in opposition to one another . . ."*(Galatians 5:17, NASB). The carnal music, together with the spiritual lyrics, is a "picture" of this scriptural truth.

A few verses later (Galatians 5:19) we're given a list of "sensual" sins which are considered works of the flesh.

Clearly, sensual (carnal) techniques—even in Christian music—are a work of our *flesh*, not of our spirit, and we cannot experience "pureness of spirit" in its fullest sense if we're satisfying our flesh through carnal Christian music.

This pureness, or cleanness, we experience when we listen to good music cannot be of our own making. It's a gift, like the cleanness we feel when we experience forgiveness of sin. It's *evidence* that the Holy Spirit is bearing witness with our spirits that the music is good.[7] Many times we may feel in our hearts an overwhelming gratefulness and love to God. This isn't to be confused with those moments of pureness that God gives us. And *in no way* am I suggesting that we're to seek any sort of "feeling"—energetic or otherwise—when we worship God. We worship out of obedience, gratefulness, and love for Him. What I *am* saying is that when we *are* "inspired" during worship, it should come from God. Our inspiration should *not* arise from our (carnal) response to the unnatural rhythms and/or sensual sounds of carnal music.

The Christian walk is a walk of faith, not of feelings. Furthermore, if we are to worship God according to the verse, *"God is a Spirit: and they that worship him must worship him in spirit and in truth"* (John 4:24), we shouldn't be using carnal music to help us "feel" spiritual. That isn't being *truthful* in our worship. Carnal music is an artificial method of obtaining "feelings" of spirituality. Those feelings are not true spirituality: they're actually a carnal response to the carnal music.

Therefore, carnal music in worship doesn't equal truth in worship. If Jesus Christ is *in* us[8] through the indwelling of the Holy Spirit, we're to *"consider the members of* [our] *earthly body as* dead [to carnality]..." (Colossians 3:5,

NASB, emphasis added). How can one be "dead to self" in Christ and at the *same time* satisfy the flesh through music's carnal rhythms? He can't! Honestly, would Jesus Christ puposely listen to any music containing devices that appeal to the "flesh"—however subtle those (sensual) devices may be? Would He be glorified through music that contains carnal and/or sensual elements?

When we come to worship knowing that we should be "dead" to ourselves, yet (knowingly or unknowingly) participate in carnal music, we're not being truthful with ourselves, nor with God, and we're not fully worshipping a Holy God "in spirit and in truth."

Music is a powerful tool. This is one reason our music (both the lyrics and the "vehicle") should be Godly—to ensure that we're responding to the right sort of stimuli in a manner pleasing to God.

Another thing to keep in mind is the legacy we're leaving to our children and to generations to follow. Are we willing to be looked upon as that generation that allowed carnal music into the Church and into our Christian culture as a whole? On the contrary, it's imperative that we set an example, preserving Godly music now and for the Church to come. *Simply stated, rock music, "Christian" or otherwise, is not our Christian musical heritage.* Just as the Great Revivals led to a massive return to God's Word and an understanding of His holiness, so also if the Church today were to experience persecution or "fiery trials," or even widespread national catastrophe, no doubt there would be a massive return to our *Godly* musical heritage as well.

God wants us to worship Him in *His* way, not our way. Remember in the Old Testament when He instructed His people to destroy the idolatrous altars?[9] They were perfectly good altars; why couldn't the people use them? But God said no, they were to *completely* eliminate the idolatrous altars and eventually build *new* altars.

God has already given us suitable music through which to worship Him. When man begins to use his own reasoning and imitate the music that comes out of the world's system, he has, in effect, done the same that God's people of the Old Testament would have done if they had used the idolatrous altars in their worship. We cannot mix the world's ways with God's requirement for worship—which should be *unspotted* from the world.

I'm not saying we need to "throw out the baby with the bathwater." It *is* possible, in most cases, to retain many of the recently written beautiful melodies and meaningful Christian lyrics and eliminate unnatural rhythms and/or other sensual techniques.

Here's where the rubber meets the road: How deep is our commitment to God? Either we're going to follow Him in every way, to the best of our ability, or we aren't. God's Word commands: *"Thou shalt love the Lord thy God with* all *thy heart, and with* all *thy soul, and with* all *thy strength, and with* all *thy mind . . ."* (Deuteronomy 6:5; Luke 10:27, emphasis added).

Music is an area in our lives that needs to be seriously evaluated. Satan has used contemporary Christian music to lead astray many young people who were once fully committed to the Lord,[10] and he has blinded many other believers as well. Where other devices have failed, Satan's craftiness in deceiving us through contemporary Christian music has infiltrated the Church to the point that we now wholeheartedly embrace it. We *must* reclaim the ground we've given so that we may be effective witnesses for the Lord Jesus Christ.

Yes, the music we listen to does make a difference, and it's time to take responsibility for the type of music we listen to and sing. It's time to be discerning and to no longer be led astray, as if blindfolded. We must draw a line at where the world ends and where we as Christians begin. As in any other area of life, we cannot compromise.

Yet we *are* compromising when we hold on to our questionable music. Little do we realize that we are, in fact, serving a different "master" when we claim that it's only the words of a song that we listen to, not the music. If this isn't the case, why are we so adamant about retaining the (carnal) music to which those words are sung? And if we think certain music is "boring" (such as traditional hymns), then we have just admitted that it *is* those unnatural rhythms that appeal to us, *not* the words! Obviously, the music has some hold over us—and therefore the carnal music *has* become our "master."

Matthew 6:24 says,

"No man can serve two masters: for either he will hate the one, and love the other; or else he will hold to the one, and despise the other. Ye cannot serve God and mammon (emphasis added)."

Which master will you and I serve?

CHAPTER ELEVEN

THE PATH OF DECLINE

"...Every man did that which was right in his own eyes."

Judges 17:6

There's an old saying that goes something like this: "To know where you're going, you've got to know where you've been." We've come a long way since the music of our Western civilization began. To go forward, we need to look back so we can understand, and then apply, the wisdom we gain. We need to turn our attention to our collective Christian response concerning our musical heritage as it has progressed, and the ramifications of those responses.

When Jesus left the earth, one of the last things He said was, *"Go ye therefore, and teach all nations...."*[1] With the spreading of the Gospel, it is natural that methods of worship—including the types of songs they sang—were also spread. We've seen that the music of Western civilization began in the early Christian Church. Was this by accident? And were subsequent developments of the hymn chorales by accident or chance? It's *obvious* that God's hand directed these advancements in Christian music.

As the Gospel spread across the European continent and then to the Americas, Godly music spread as well. Those who were converted to Christianity adopted the Church's music. It's only fitting that the new converts looked to the wiser Christians for guidance; it would have been foolish for the younger in Christ to tell the more spiritually mature how to conduct their lives and worship services.

In this country the African slaves were exposed to the Gospel. It should be noted that as they developed their own form of worship music (spirituals), they patterned it after the Protestant hymns—without taking away the African's natural and unique freedom of expression. Moreover, those original spirituals were *not* accompanied by instruments of music other than hand-clapping and foot-stomping.[2*]

Everyone was still on-track concerning acceptable Christian church music as it developed from the early Church, and then, the Reformation.

Then secular rock music entered the picture. For a time, the Church kept the traditional music that had been passed down through the ages. As time passed, our defenses were slowly eroded and we became accustomed to these "new sounds." We allowed our standards to be lowered, and then we accepted those lower standards. Young Christian songwriters began to follow this new trend, calling the new religious music "Jesus Music."[4] The Church began (and continues) to imitate the world's music, disregarding several facts, some of which we've already discussed:

1. Rock music was created by ungodly people who were intent on demonstrating rebellion. *God's Word states: "For*

rebellion is as the sin of witchcraft..." (I Samuel 15:23). Witchcraft is an *abomination* in the sight of God, therefore so is rebellion.

2. By adopting the world's music, which not only is rebellious but was influenced by pagan rhythms, God's command in Jeremiah 10:2 to *"learn not the way of the heathen"* has been ignored on two points:

a) the fact that rock music had, from its inception, incorporated pagan rhythms into its context,

b) the fact that the Christians are now imitating the world's (heathen/carnal) music.

3. The Bible is clear: Believers are to sing *non-carnal songs.* (See Ephesians 5:19 and Colossians 3:16.) Paul outlined three types of acceptable music for the Church, and "spiritual songs"—music other than hymns or psalms—is not a new concept. There are limitations: *any* music is not acceptable. If it was important enough to mention to the early Church, how much *more* relevant are these verses today when we have added so much to our music by way of harmony and instrumentation?

4. Those who like the new contemporary religious music are the younger ones in the churches. Now the younger in Christ are telling the elders how to conduct the services. No one listens to the elders, who have more spiritual maturity and are offended by this music. In Scripture, the elders are *always* revered.

5. Acceptance of the new (carnal) music follows the same pattern we follow when we become ensnared in any sin. (More on this later.)

6. Scriptural principles are violated in the mixture of carnal music with Christian lyrics.

101

The first principle is that darkness and light cannot mix. So many times Scripture talks about darkness and light.[5] The darkness represents our old way of life—a life of sin and spiritual blindness. The light is our new life in Christ Jesus. Apply this analogy to Christian rock music and the similarities are quickly evident. The rock beat came out of a lifestyle of sin and spiritual blindness (darkness). The Christian lyrics represent light and spiritual newness. Yet, the Bible says, "...*What fellowship has light with darkness?*"[6] If we're true Christians, we can't "straddle the fence" by walking half in darkness and half in light. But that's *exactly* what listening to Christian rock music causes us to do. Ephesians 5:8 tells us to "...*walk as children of light.*" Shouldn't our music also evidence this pureness?

Living the Christian life isn't a question of how *close* we can get to the "line" between the world's ways and acceptable Christian living. It's a matter of how *far away* from that line we can get in order to be a true beacon of light in a dark world. The closer to the world's way we drift—without actually "crossing the line"—the dimmer our "beacon" will grow.

The beacon of a lighthouse stands out with such brilliance that it cannot be missed. It also guides ships to safety. When religious music sounds like the world's carnal music, how are we exhibiting the characteristics of a beacon with our music? To fully examine the word *sound*, we must take into consideration the full range of the sound—not just the lyrics. Isn't the music (which supports those lyrics) making a "sound" as well? If we're to fully "walk in light," how can religious music use *any* sounds of darkness?

Christian rock music doesn't just come "close" to the line between light and darkness—it actually *crosses* the line because it imitates music that came out of spiritual darkness. It did not retain the pure heritage of religious music's development through classical music and hymns, which were inspired through Christian men and which began in the early Christian Church. The Bible commands us in Ephesians 5:11 to *"...have no fellowship with the unfruitful works of darkness, but rather reprove them."* Most certainly, rock music was, and is, an "unfruitful work of darkness" and should not be emulated by Christians.

Another principle is that an immoral lifestyle and a pure life cannot mix. The Bible is very clear about immorality.[7] Because rock music makes "sensual" sounds, it represents an immoral lifestyle. Christian lyrics represent a pure lifestyle. Are we to mix the two lifestyles? It's ridiculous to even ask! But that's what's evident in the music when we mix unnatural rhythms and sensual sounds with Christian lyrics. Many people question the truth of this. But in other art forms, would Christians mix the two?

In literary art, we read either clean books or immoral books. The same is true in the visual arts—paintings and photographs are either pure or immoral. And what about dance? It is either wholesome or sensual (immoral). For some reason, we excuse music from this critique. It's "relative," we say. In other words, we all have different "tastes" in music. Let's examine this idea of . . .

Relativism

Person A perceives that person B's music is sensual and wrong.

Person B perceives that person C's music is sensual and wrong.

Person C perceives that person D's music is sensual and wrong.

103

Who's right? We see that there are varying "degrees" of rock musical styles and varying degrees of their acceptability. To God, evil is evil. Wrong is wrong. There are no "degrees" of evil. Something is either wrong or it isn't. To make this a bit more clear, let's look at the life of an immoral person.

An immoral person is comfortable with his lifestyle and sees no wrong in it. His conscience has been dulled. That person may participate in a little immorality, or a lot. Just as one immoral person may be "comfortable" with only a "little" immorality, so someone else may be comfortable practicing "hard-core" immorality. There are varying degrees. Where do we draw the line? Obviously, at *no* immorality.

Rock music (Christian or otherwise) is the same. There are varying degrees of "impurity." However, when we seek to draw a line, everyone holds on to *his* "area of comfort." We claim it's all relative. We claim we're all individuals.

In reality, our consciences have been dulled in our "area," just as the immoral person's conscience has been dulled.

What we're doing when we say music is a matter of personal preference—relativism—is *establishing ourselves as the authority on what's best for us.* We have mocked God and set for ourselves our own standards, and these standards will be different for each and every one of us. Ultimately, Scripture, and scriptural principles, will no longer be our "plumb line." We'll judge matters by how we personally feel.

This argument, "I *feel* closer to God when I listen to music that pleases me," is the same rationalization as the secular mantra, "If it feels good, do it." God doesn't ask us to "feel good" about anything. God wants us to obey, which sometimes calls for denial of ourselves (and our musical preferences).

How did we come to accept Christian rock music?

We've discussed before that when rock music first emerged, we were shocked. That should have been our first indication that it was wrong. Hearing it over and over dulled our senses and broke down our natural, God-given resistance.

When the rock beat was put into religious music (and named "Jesus Music" and later, Contemporary Christian), many Christians—particularly the older, wiser Christians—had "cautions" about it. Then we started justifying: "They're having fun!" "The words are great!" "It appeals to the young people!" Etc., etc.

We listened a little longer. What once seemed clearly wrong soon became, "This isn't so bad!" And after awhile *it became acceptable without reservations.*

This pattern works across the board—from "soft" Christian rock to Christian rap. *Anything experienced over and over becomes acceptable after a time.*

We fail to realize that this pattern—caution, justification, less caution, acceptance without reservations—is the *same pattern* we go through when we get into bondage to sin.

Is it bondage? Yes. Rock music (even Christian rock music) creates a stronghold[8] similar to that which alcohol creates in an alcoholic. Just as an alcoholic denies he's an alcoholic, so those who listen to rock music, "Christian" or otherwise, will *deny* there's a problem with the music. Try to stop listening to it for an extended length of time. It will be evident that the music is a dominant force in life.

How are alcoholics helped? By total abstinence, and it's a difficult thing to accomplish, especially in the first thirty days.

What does the Christian do when he truly wants to seek God's will? He fasts, prays, and studies the Scriptures. If we're really serious about seeking God on this issue, it behooves us to test the music by removing *all* questionable music (take a "music fast") for at least one month—better, two. If there's a problem in identifying such music, ask a respected elder who is known for his stand on Godly music.

During this "fast" listen only to hymns that are played in the *traditional* style, or classical music. Suggestions for listening are also listed at the end of this book (Appendix One).

After our time of seeking God and being apart from the questionable music, our ability to identify out-of-balance rhythms will be improved because our ears will have been "retrained." The conflicting rhythms and sensual sounds will become more apparent, and our natural, God-given "caution" (concerning music) will have returned because, just as a physical fast from food cleanses the body, so a fast from carnal music sharpens our "ears," as well as enhances our spiritual discernment in the area of music.

Won't God honor our music fast? We'll have demonstrated that we're serious about finding His will, instead of simply *assuming* what His will is on this issue.

Until we're ready to get serious about seeking God by observing a music fast, we'll develop our own convictions about the music we listen to.

Convictions

Everyone talks about conviction. Actually, there are two types of conviction, and the dictionary defines them both:

1. The act of convicting or condition of being con-
victed. 2. A strong opinion or belief.[9]

In the Christian realm, the first definition applies to us
when God is doing the convicting, such as bringing a person to repentance for a particular sin. The second definition is what we *personally* believe, whether or not those
beliefs are based on Scripture, or scriptural principles. Unfortunately, we use the second definition interchangeably
with the first. We say, "My conviction about [music] is
that . . ." when we *really* should say, "My *opinion* about
[music] is that...." Yet we use the first statement because it
sounds like our "conviction" is from God. When our conviction is from God, it will be to show us our sin. If we have
a belief *based on Scripture*, it will be a *scriptural conviction*.
Anything else is just an opinion.

So now we apply this to music. We *must* ask ourselves,
"What is my *scriptural* conviction about music?" Any other
question, without basing the answer on Scripture, falls short
of Godly standards and is merely an opinion.

We can't assume that because the Bible says nothing
about rock music it's okay. Isn't God such an all-knowing
God that He knew rock music and every other kind of carnal music would be part of history? And when He revealed
the Scriptures, didn't He intend for His revealed Word to
cover *every* aspect of our Christian lives? The Bible is written on various levels. Some things are straightforward—
the "milk" of the Word. Other things are "meat." The most
precious times are when we search for the "meat" in His
Word.

Why should we expect "Divine Revelation" about anything when God has already addressed it in Scripture?

Is God interested in the type of music we listen to?

Of course. *It is a form of worship.* And, as such, it should be as undefiled as possible, to the best of our earthly ability.

I Corinthians 10:31 says, *"...Whatsoever ye do, do all to the glory of God."* The *Ryrie Study Bible* comments that this means we should "...test all conduct by whether or not it manifests the characteristics of God."[10] Our musical listening and singing habits certainly qualify as "conduct."

What are the characteristics of God? We've already mentioned that God is a God of order. He is also pure (no darkness, only light).[11] Holy (commands our respect). He's the same yesterday, today, and forever. (He remains unaffected by cultural change.)[12] And there are many other characteristics that apply to God. So we should ask, "Is the music I listen to orderly? Is it pure and holy? Is it unaffected by cultural change?" (This doesn't mean we can't express ourselves with new music and lyrics. It *does* mean that the cultural "whims" should not dictate or compromise our Godly musical styles.)

Ryrie goes on to comment that other principles in I Corinthians should also guide our conduct as believers, and these can be applied to the music we listen to:[13]

1. Is it beneficial? (I Corinthians 6:12)
2. Is it enslaving? (I Corinthians 6:12)
3. Will it hinder the spiritual growth of a brother? (I Corinthians 8:13)
4. Does it edify (build up)? (I Corinthians 10:23)

Let's look at these briefly:

1. "Is [the music] beneficial?" This is a hard one to apply, because some people will say yes, some no. We have to research further than our own "opinion" and apply other biblical principles that we've learned.

2. "Is [the music] enslaving?" We've touched upon this already in this chapter.

③ "Will [the music] hinder the spiritual growth of a brother?" This could also be combined with, "Will it offend another believer?"[14]

4. "Does [the music] edify?" Recalling chapter four—the study on biblical references to music—not only should we judge the lyrics but also the musical "vehicle." We can't ignore one for the other. What if we switched the two, so that the music was fine but the lyrics were ungodly? The argument that the "whole" edifies—or that we're not listening to the words but still feel drawn to God through the music—now seems ludicrous.

Because we are to consider the whole counsel of Scripture, we cannot lift one of these principles and stake our claim that it justifies our music. *Every single principle* must be applied so that we can answer with an unreserved "Yes! The music I listen to follows the principles of Scripture."

To help us answer in the affirmative, here are some...

Questions to think about in your own life
1. What are my *scriptural convictions* (beliefs based on Scripture) concerning music?
2. Does the music I listen to enable me to comply with each and every principle Paul has outlined in I Corinthians (and any other principles in Scripture)?
3. Have I truly sought God with a music fast, prayer, and Bible study?
4. Have I established myself or God's Word as the authority concerning the music I listen to?
5. Can I truly say I'm singing/listening to non-carnal music as directed in Ephesians 5:19 and Colossians 3:16?
6. Might this music offend an elder in the church?
7. Does the music I listen to exhibit the characteristics of God?

8. Am I willing to give up any offensive or questionable music?

God is waiting for us to seek His will and obey Him *completely*. If we choose a path that's not in complete obedience, it doesn't mean He won't bless or use us. It only means that we'll never know (in this life) what *His best* for us would have been, and some of our choices may actually hinder our witness for Christ.

Nevertheless, this shouldn't be an excuse to avoid seeking God in any area of our lives, including our music. When we're given new insights—through whatever avenue—we'll be held accountable for what we *do* with those insights.

By imitating the ungodly, carnal styles of music and adapting them to religious music, we've chosen a path that isn't in complete obedience to God's Word. But the last chapter has not yet been played out on earth. If we turn back to the right path, there's hope that we will still receive God's *best*, and He will give us "beauty for ashes."[15]

May the Lord God guide each and every one of us as we search for music that is "good and true and pure."[16]

Chapter Eleven Notes

[*] Putting movements to music was a natural expression of the African's life.[3] It was their culture and heritage. This brings us to the point that there are *many* cultures, each with different practices. Each is unique. It's important that Christians in *all* cultures define their own beliefs and practices (dancing, music, etc.) *within their particular culture and according to Scripture.*

God doesn't change Scripture for each culture. The beautiful reality is that Scripture, and scriptural principles, *will* apply to *every* culture.

CHAPTER TWELVE

A NEW SONG

"Let your light so shine before men, that they may see your good works, and glorify your Father which is in heaven."

Matthew 5:16

One of the good works others can see most readily in our lives is our music. Our music gives us an opportunity to be a light in this world so that we may bring hope to others through Jesus Christ our Lord.

This book has given us a new standard for music—a biblical standard. Yet because of our human nature, along with our personal backgrounds and long-entrenched habits, we may find it difficult to accept. Life for the Christian seems to always be an uphill struggle. Not one of us will ever be perfect until we're united with our Lord Jesus Christ.

God is gracious as He looks upon our human weaknesses. Yet He gently encourages us toward complete surrender in order to be like Christ, for therein He knows is the secret to our true joy and happiness as believers.

As I was putting this last chapter together, I came upon a note I had written in my Bible, from a sermon by a well-known and respected preacher. My note said, "We must view things from our spirit, not mind. Many things our mind will accept, the spirit won't. *Ask* the Holy Spirit—He will give the ability to discern truth from error in our spirit."[1]

One doesn't have to be a music scholar to be able to discern music with one's spirit. We need to trust the initial impression the Lord gives us, instead of rationalizing or justifying the music's content. We must discern with our spirits, not justify with our minds.

Discerning with our spirits means pausing a moment to listen for God's direction with out hearts and minds, to… "wait on the Lord."[2] The answer won't necessarily be audible, as in words, but there will be either a check or a caution in our spirits, or a peace that all is well.

To aid our discernment, it's essential that we retrain our "ears" (both physical and spiritual) by observing a music fast, as discussed in the previous chapter. Why? If the Holy Spirit has been "quenched"[3] (in regard to music) because of our previous desensitization to unnatural rhythms, we have to establish a *new* level of sensitivity. This is accomplished through a music fast, Bible study, and prayer.

In the Old Testament, King Solomon prayed this prayer: *"Give therefore thy servant an understanding heart to judge thy people, that I may discern between good and bad . . ."* (I Kings 3:9). We can use this as a pattern for our prayer concerning music: "Lord, give me an understanding heart to judge music, so that I may be able to discern between good and bad." Additionally, the Bible says in John 16:13 that the Holy Spirit "...*will guide you into all truth.*" Let's ask Him to guide us into the truth about music, so that we may be obedient in this important aspect of our lives. Let's ask Him to give us the will and strength to obey.

An essential concept to grasp is this: If our heart's desire is complete obedience to God, then *we are free to exercise our personal preferences only after we have obeyed biblical principles.* For example, the biblical principle of dressing modestly can be observed, while at the same time we're free to choose the color and style of our clothing. If the style we choose doesn't follow biblical principles, we've made a wrong choice. The same with music. There are some "styles" that do not follow biblical principles. Every facet of life must follow this pattern—even those areas which at first glance appear "gray." It's then our responsibility to prayerfully search out those areas in Scripture to the point where we *know* we're following scriptural principles, remembering that we cannot take *one* principle (or Scripture) and rest on it to support our preference, but acknowledge that any principle will always line up with the *whole* counsel of Scripture. We may prefer a certain type of music, but in all things we're to submit to God;[4] over time He will change our preference.

The Bible is our textbook for life, and without following scriptural principles we fall prey to humanistic philosophies.

My intention is not to witch hunt. Neither should we strain at a gnat when we hear songs that may be questionable but aren't sure because there's no clear-cut evidence either way. *We can listen "too hard" and miss a meaningful message*. And remember, an occasional accented offbeat does not a rock song make! We should merely avoid the obvious, relying on God to help us discern the questionable. "If in doubt, don't." And we should be gracious towards those who are trying their best with all of their heart, just as God is gracious toward us as we ourselves struggle.

My goal is to encourage each of us to be more aware and discerning of the music we listen to and sing, so that, in obedience, we may bring before a Holy God "good and true and pure" music that is worthy of Him. I hope this has been accomplished. There *are* many wonderful and uplifting songs out there, and they're not all funeral dirges!

Are we willing to "let go" of unscriptural musical practices? Are we ready to get serious about God's holiness? Are we ready for a deeper walk with the Lord Jesus Christ?

The Bible speaks nine times of a "new" song. In each case it's a "fresh, new thing."[5] In this era, when there are so many voices calling to us to follow their way, won't you, with me, *"come out from among them and be separate"*?[6]

Together, we'll sing a new song.

> *"For the Father up above is looking down in love,*
> *So be careful little ears what you hear."*

APPENDIX ONE

SUGGESTIONS FOR LISTENING

It's good to begin to replace our old habits with new and better habits so there won't be a void. Listening to only good music also helps us train our ears so that when we encounter bad music, we recognize it immediately. This is much like filling our minds with Scripture so we can discern truth from error.

Obviously, one can't review every album in existence. The following selections, however, are "good and true and pure" music. (I haven't listed every song on each album—only key, representative pieces.)*

Pure Classical

From The Masterpiece Collection: The following are nice introductions to classical composers. I've chosen three to list; other composers are also available in this collection.

• *Johann Sebastian Bach: Volume I.* This contains the famous Toccata and Fugue in D Minor (for organ), as well as selections for strings, piano, and orchestra.
• *George Friedrich Handel.* Includes works from *The Messiah* ("Hallelujah Chorus," plus two more); *Water Music; Fireworks Music.*
• *Antonio Vivaldi.* Probably best known for his *Four Seasons*, which is featured on this album.

(The Masterpiece Collection is produced by Regency Music, Nashville, TN.)

Contemporary Classical

By "contemporary classical" I mean music that has been written relatively recently yet follows the classical styles of Western civilization. It also includes classical or folk pieces that have been updated yet remain classical in form.

Anne, by Hagood Hardy. This is the original music score from the films *Anne of Green Gables* and *Anne of Avonlea*. Beautiful.

Piano Reflections, performed by Kelly Yost. Gentle, soothing recordings of classical music pieces such as Debussy's "Reverie"; Saint-Saens' "The Swan"; and a Brahms waltz, as well as a few contemporary classical selections.

Roses and Solitude, also performed by Kelly Yost. Albums by Kelly "appeal to both the connoisseur of fine music and the listener who didn't even know they liked classical music." This album includes Rachmaninoff's Eighteenth Variation from Rhapsodie on a Theme of Paganini.

The Water Is Wide, by Mark Small and Robert Torres. Two guitars and a Chamber Ensemble (flute, oboe, English horn, and strings) perform reflective classical pieces, as well as contemporary classical. At times melancholic, but mostly very nice, with two hymns: "Abide With Me" and "Jesu, Joy of Man's Desiring."

NOTE: Sometimes these four albums are mistakenly placed in the New Age display in music stores; however, they are truly classical, or contemporary classical.

(The above selections are produced by Channel Productions, 305 3rd Ave. E., P.O. Box 454, Twin Falls, ID 83303-0454, phone: 208-734-8668.)

Religious: Instrumental
Ambience, for piano. (Other instruments are also available.) These are very soothing and gentle hymns done in a contemporary classical arrangement for piano with light orchestra. Unobtrusive, yet wonderful.

Celtic Hymns, with instruments of Ireland, Scotland, and Wales. This is delightful, a bit "different" to the ear. British Isles folk-type music, with both toe-tapping and meditative hymns, make this an excellent and joyous album. "All Things Bright and Beautiful," "Be Thou My Vision," "Amazing Grace," other lesser known hymns, and one vocal: "Joys Seven."

Hymnworks, Volumes I and II, performed and arranged by Linda McKechnie, piano, with the Don Marsh orchestra. These are contemporary classical arrangements of hymns, interwoven with classical pieces to create inspiring, uplifting, and exciting musical listening. (These would be my first choice.)
• Volume I: "'Tis so Sweet to Trust in Jesus" (interwoven with "Claire de Lune," by Debussy), "Fairest Lord Jesus" (with "Jesu, Joy of Man's Desiring," by Bach), "When I Survey the Wondrous Cross" (with "Air" by Bach), plus seven more

117

• Volume II: "To God Be the Glory (with Concerto No. 1, by Tchaikovsky), O the Deep, Deep Love of Jesus (with "Moonlight Sonata," by Beethoven), "Holy, Holy, Holy" (with Piano Concerto No. 2, by Rachmaninoff), plus seven more.

(*Ambience* and *Celtic Hymns* are produced by Brentwood Music, Inc., Brentwood, TN.

Hymnworks are produced by Don Marsh, Brentwood Music, Inc., Brentwood, TN.)

Religious: Choral

Hymns Triumphant, Volumes I and II, with the London Philharmonic Choir and the National Philharmonic Orchestra. These are outstanding! Hymns done in a truly exalted style.

• Volume I: Medleys of forty-two traditional hymns, including, "O Sacred Head-Were You There-When I Survey the Wondrous Cross" and "Amazing Grace-Jesus Lover of My Soul-Just as I Am."

• Volume II: More hymn-medleys: "There Is a Fountain-Alas, and Did My Savior Bleed-What Wondrous Love Is This"; "I Will Arise and Go to Jesus-How Firm a Foundation-It Is Well With My Soul"; and many others.

He Cares for You, by Frank Garlock, with The Men of Praise. These are timeless, inspiring messages of faith. "He Cares for You," "Fill My Cup, Lord," "Until Then," plus nine more titles.

(*Hymns Triumphant* are produced by The Sparrow Corporation, Brentwood, TN.

He Cares for You is produced by Majesty Music, Greenville, SC.)

Solo Recordings

Moments, Volume I, by George Beverly Shea. An album for the entire family. Titles include: "The Wonder of It All," "How Great Thou Art," and "This Little Light of Mine."

Rejoice in the Lord, by Ron Hamilton. A wonderful album, also for every member of the family. "Christ Is Coming," "It is Finished," and the children will love "Jonah." Seven more songs.

NOTE: Majesty Music has many more recordings—solo, duet, choral, orchestral, and instrumental, as well as music books and teaching supplies. This company can be trusted for uplifting and Godly music. Their address and phone number will be listed under the viewing section.

(*Moments, Volume I* produced by Star Song Communications.

Rejoice in the Lord produced by Majesty Music, Greenville, SC.)

Children

Patch the Pirate series, by Ron and Shelly Hamilton. Through fun music and special sound effects, Christian "pirate," Captain Patch, leads children on character-building adventures combined with biblical messages. Album story-titles include *Mount Zion Marathon, Harold the King, Down Under* and many others.

Why Can't I See God? by Judy Rogers. Pure and simple music that addresses children's questions about God and the Bible. Nice for bedtime listening. Some of the titles: "The Salvation Song," "God Is a Spirit," "The Ten Commandments," plus eighteen more.

(*Patch the Pirate* series produced by Majesty Music.

Why Can't I See God? produced by Judy Rogers, Atlanta, GA.)

For Viewing

The Language of Music, by Dr. Frank Garlock, of Majesty Music. A six-tape set that presents scriptural principles concerning music. Titles of the series: "The God of Music," "The Message of Music," "The Sound of Music," "The Gospel of Music," "The Effects of Music," "The Purpose of Music." This would be a great six-week course for churches. All types of music are discussed so that discernment of music may be achieved. Highly recommended.

NOTE: Dr. Garlock also has a book, *Music in the Balance*, coauthored by Kurt Woetzel, which combines scriptural principles with insights from various communication and musical scholars. Recommended reading. Contact Majesty Music, Box 6524, Greenville, SC 29606, phone: 1-800-334-1071.

Wildlife Fantasia, by Reader's Digest. This is wonderful. Watch wildlife in their beautiful habitats—set to music by some of the great classical composers. Fifteen selections.

Appendix One Notes

* NOTE: Unless otherwise noted, listing of a specific album does not necessarily endorse every album produced by a performer or publishing company.

APPENDIX TWO

CHRISTIAN MUSIC COMPARISON CHART

Contemporary Christian (unnatural rhythms, etc.)	Godly Christian (straightforward rhythms)
1. Disorderly. (I Corinthians 14:33)	1. Orderly. (I Corinthians 14:40)
2. Rhythms originated from pagan culture. (Jeremiah 10:2; Romans 8:7)	2. Religious music of Western civilization originated in New Testament church. (Ephesians 5:19; Colossians 3:16)

3. Appeals to the flesh. (Romans 8:6a; 8:8)	3. Appeals to the spirit. (John 4:23–24; Romans 8:6b)
4. "Pictures" conflict of our spirit with our old sin-nature. (Romans 7:14–25; Galatians 5:17)	4. Pure; "pictures" denial of sin nature and self-control. (Romans 8:12–14; Galatians 5:22–25)
5. "Tickles" the ears to draw people to the church. (II Timothy 4:3)	5. Acknowledges that it is God, through the Holy Spirit, Who draws people to Christ. (John 6:44)
6. Imitation of the world. (I John 2:15)	6. Separateness from the world. (Romans 12:2; II Corinthians 6:14-17)
7. Use of "sensual" techniques. (I John 2:16)	7. No such techniques used. Morally righteous. (Romans 13:14; I Peter 1:15-16)
8. Contributes to emotionalism in worship. (John 4:23–24; I Corinthians 14:33)	8. Encourages true, Spirit-filled worship. (John 4:23–24; Philippians 3:3)

Scripture references are not exhaustive. See II Timothy 3:16–17.

APPENDIX THREE

CARNAL MUSIC TECHNIQUES

This appendix is to be used as a starting point for identifying and discerning sensual elements in music. New techniques may be developed, but they can all be evaluated by our asking ourselves, "How is this music affecting my body?" Do we merely want to tap our toes along with the *melody's* rhythm—perhaps even think of a folk-type dance or march (good music)? Or does our body want to respond with a "thrust" of the head, shoulder or hip? (This response could either be to an *additional* rhythm, a "teasing" rhythm, or even a strong, *unnatural* rhythm of a melody.) Does the music create a subtle, sensual sound? These are indications that the music is appealing to the flesh and is therefore carnal.

1. *Offbeat accents.* These are accents—usually on the second and fourth beats—that are unrelated to the melody and may be either subtle (quiet) or driving (loud and forceful). They will be continuous throughout a portion of the music, or throughout the entire piece, always played by a drum or bass guitar or, sometimes, a cymbal. This is the "classic" rock musical style.

2. *Any rhythm that conflicts with the melody.* The melody should always be priority, with no rhythm conflicting against it or dominating the music.

3. *Swing rhythms.* These evoke a sense or feeling of "da, dah, da, dah, dah" (the "Big Band" sound). Also, any rhythm or melody in which beats seem to be held slightly longer than necessary ("teasing")—boogie-woogie, jazz, "cool," etc.

4. *An unnatural rhythm that has no melody.* Usually solely drums, sometimes with cymbals or other percussive devices added. This is a strong, rhythmic piece of "music" that evokes carnal body movements.

5. *"Rhythm melodies" that are obviously based on strong, repetitive, unnatural rhythm patterns.* These can be played by a single instrument or an entire band. Some examples include calypso music and strong jazz or rock music. These types of "rhythm melodies" also cause our torsos to respond in carnal movements.

6. *Sliding or scooping.* Used mainly by vocalists and jazz musicians. This technique is achieved by "sliding" down

from one note to a lower note, or "scooping" up from a lower note to a higher note. The "slide" or "scoop" can pass through any number of notes between the starting note and the ending note. For example, the "scoop" could go from one note to the note next to it on the musical scale, or it could go an entire octave (eight notes) or more. Also included in this technique is the practice of landing briefly on the note just below what is written in the music, and then "scooping" up to the intended note.

NOTE: A similar musical technique used in operatic (and classical) music is called a *glissando*; however, because the operatic vocalist makes a (brief) distinction of each note that is passed over, the glissando isn't sensual.

7. *Breathiness or gravelliness.* Used by vocalists.

8. *"Sensual" vibrato.* Vibrato is slight fluctuation in the pitch of a note being held for any length of time. It becomes sensual when the fluctuation is "slowed." Used by vocalists and jazz musicians.

9. *Dissonances.* Tense, unresolved-sounding chords or other techniques that are "grating" to the ears.

ENDNOTES

Foreword
 1. John 4:24.

Chapter One
 1. Galatians 5:25.
 2. Romans 13:14.
 3. Ephesians 5:19; Colossians 3:16.
 4. Amos 3:3.
 5. Charles Stanley, *How to Listen to God*, p. 56.

Chapter Two
 1. Program: "Musical Evening on Palace Green." Colonial Williamsburg; Williamsburg, VA. October 16, 1996.
 2. Beatrice Landeck, *Echoes of Africa in Folk Songs of the Americas*, p. 133.
 3. Ibid., p. 13.
 4. Ibid., p. 7.
 5. Ibid., p. 7–9.
 6. Ibid., p. 3.
 7. Ibid., p. 130.
 8. Ibid. NOTE: It is doubtful that the banning of drums was strictly adhered to in every area of the South.

9. Ibid.
10. The original spirituals sung by the slaves were essentially only a "*framework* for solo improvisations and group responses." (Ibid., p. 130.) The spirituals as we know them are more restrained, as they have been "Westernized."
11. "Gospel music," *The 1995 Grolier Multimedia Encyclopedia.* Courtesy, Grolier Interactive, Inc.
12. Landeck, p. 131.
13. Ibid.
14. Ibid., pp. 131–132.
15. Dan Peters and Steve Peters, *Why Knock Rock?* p. 13.
16. Landeck, p. 133.
17. Ibid. The term "rock and roll" has also been described as a "sexual metaphor." Peters, p. 13.
18. Peters, p. 13.
19. Landeck., p. 133.
20. Ibid., p. 136.
21. Jerry M. Grigadean, "Rock Music," *The World Book Encyclopedia*, 1989, Vol. 16, p. 383.

Chapter Three
1. "Rock of Ages," words, Augustus M. Toplady; music, Thomas Hastings.
2. *humneo* (5214), Strong, Greek lexicon, p. 73.
3. *The American Heritage Dictionary*, p. 476. Copyright ©1983 by Houghton Mifflin Company. Adapted and reproduced by permission from *The American Heritage Dictionary, Second Paperback Edition.*
4. Leonard W. Van Camp, "Hymn," *The World Book Encyclopedia*, 1989, Vol. 9, p. 458.
5. Source: Lecture, *Church Music in the Colonies.* David J. De Simone, Religion Historian. Colonial Williamsburg; Williamsburg, VA. October 16, 1996.

6. S. M. Houghton, *Sketches from Church History*, p. 186.
7. Ibid.
8. Albert Edward Bailey, *The Gospel in Hymns*, p. 49.
9. Leonard W. Van Camp, "Watts, Isaac," *The World Book Encyclopedia*, 1989, Vol. 21, p. 149.
10. David Lowes Watson, "Wesley, Charles," *The World Book Encyclopedia*, 1989, Vol. 21, p. 198.
11. Van Camp, "Hymn," p. 458. NOTE: Because the poetic meters of many hymn lyrics are the same, they can be sung to different hymn tunes without any difficulty. In fact, over the years, many hymns have adopted tunes that were once associated with other hymns.
12. NOTE: Although very early hymns and chorales lacked "measured time," that is, the music contained no measure notations for structured counting (as in 3/4 or 4/4 time), the rhythms were nonetheless rhythmic and orderly in the larger sense. This was in keeping with the poetic nature and cadence of the words as they progressed through all stanzas of the hymn.

Chapter Four
1. Deuteronomy 4:9; 4:15; 6:12; 8:11; 11:16; 12:30.
2. I Corinthians 10:11–12, NASB. (See also vv. 1–10.)
3. "Come Thou Fount of Every Blessing," words, Robert Robinson; music, *Nettleton*.
4. Psalm 22:3.
5. Religious music: I Chronicles 15:16; II Chronicles 7:6; Psalms 33:3; 40:3; etc. Secular music: I Samuel 18:6; Ecclesiastes 7:5; Isaiah 23:16; Amos 8:10; Luke 15:25.
6. Spiros Zodhiates, Th.D., ed. *The Complete Word Study Dictionary: New Testament*, "5215. *Humnos*," pp. 1406-7.
7. *pneumatikos* (4152), as defined and compared to *psuchikos* (5591), James Strong, *The New Strong's Exhaus-*

tive Concordance of the Bible, Greek lexicon, pp. 59 and 79.

8. Donald Jay Grout, *A History of Western Music*, pp. 12 and 27.

9. *Any* pure, "non-carnal" music will always glorify God for the simple fact that when God's ways are followed, He is glorified whether or not man acknowledges Him.

10. Romans 13:14.

Chapter Five

1. R. M. Longyear, "Music," *The World Book Encyclopedia*, 1989, Vol. 13, pp. 955–957.

2. Ibid., p. 955.

3. *The American Heritage Dictionary*, p. 206.

4. Romans 7:14–25.

5. Romans 6:19; Romans 7:14,18; Romans 8:5,6; I Corinthians 3:1–4; Galatians 5:16,17,19,24; Galatians 6:8; I Peter 2:11; I John 2:16. In the Greek, the word carnal is *sarkikos*, which is taken from the word *sarx*, meaning flesh or, by implication, human nature. (4559, 4561) Strong, Greek lexicon, p. 64.

6. This effect on our bodies is further documented in the book *Music in the Balance*, by Dr. Frank Garlock and Kurt Woetzel, pp. 41–46 and pp. 65–68.

7. Philippians 4:8, paraphrase.

Chapter Six

1. Donald Jay Grout, *A History of Western Music*, p. 2.

2. Ibid., p. 12.

3. F. E. Kirby, "Classical Music," *The World Book Encyclopedia*, 1989, Vol. 4, p. 647.

4. Grout, pp. 11–12.

5. Jane Stuart Smith and Betty Carlson, *The Gift of Music*, p. *xix*.

6. Grout, p. 25.
7. Ibid.
8. Ibid., p. 26.
9. Ibid., p. 114.
10. Ibid., p. 144.
11. Kirby, "Classical Music," p. 647.
12. Grout, p. 178.
13. Kirby, "Classical Music," p. 647.
14. Grout, p. 178.
15. Ibid., p. 207.
16. Ibid., p. 254.
17. Gerald Abraham, ed., *The New Oxford History of Music*, Vol. IV, p. 419.
18. Smith, p. *xix*.
19. The adoption of Protestant hymns by the Catholic church occurred after the Second Vatican Council, which concluded in 1965. Source: David J. De Simone, Religion Historian. Colonial Williamsburg; Williamsburg, VA.
20. There are some hymnals in use today that contain a wealth of religious music spanning several centuries— even back to the fifth century. In addition to selected hymn chorales, these hymnals include plainsong, chants, folksongs, and simple music for mass.

Chapter Seven

1. From *The Gift of Music* by Jane Stuart Smith and Betty Carlson, copyright © 1987, page 69. Used by permission of Good News Publishers/Crossway Books, Wheaton, Illinois 60187.
2. Gerald Abraham, ed., *The New Oxford History of Music*, Vol. IV, p. 419.
3. Ibid.
4. Ibid., p. 420.

5. Ibid., p. 422.

6. Smith, p. *xix*.

7. Abraham, p. 442. Quote from *Calvin, Institution Chretienne, iii*, ch. 20, pp. 31–32.

8. Smith, p. 32.

9. Ibid., p. 272.

10. Ibid., p. 38.

11. Ibid., p. 45.

12. Ibid., p. 52.

13. Ibid., p. 59–60.

14. Ibid., p. 68.

15. Ibid., pp. 103–104.

16. Ibid., p. 135.

17. Ibid., p. 137.

18. Ibid., chart, p. 276. Definition: *The American Heritage Dictionary*, p. 44.

19. Smith, pp. 245–247.

20. James Sykes, "Stravinsky, Igor F.," *The World Book Encyclopedia*, 1989, Vol. 18, p. 922.

21. Smith, p. 252.

22. Ibid., p. 258.

23. Ibid., p. 256–261.

24. Ibid., p. 69.

Chapter Eight

1. Leonard Feather and Eliot Tiegel, "Popular music," *The World Book Encyclopedia*, 1989, Vol. 15, p. 673.

2. Ibid.

3. Philippians 2:12.

4. Luke 15:25.

5. I Samuel 18:6.

6. II Corinthians 5:17, paraphrase.

7. Ephesians 2:10.

8. Texe Marrs, *Dark Secrets of the New Age*, p. ix.

9. Ibid., p. 11.
10. Ibid.
11. Ibid., p. 13.
12. Ibid., pp. 14–15, and Walter Martin, *The New Age Cult*, pp. 25–34.
13. Martin, p. 19.
14. Marrs, p. 15.
15. Douglas R. Groothuis, *Unmasking the New Age*, p. 22.
16. Marrs, p. 16.
17. Ibid.
18. "New Age music," *The 1995 Grolier Multimedia Encyclopedia.* Courtesy, Grolier Interactive, Inc.
19. Ibid.
20. "New Age," *The 1995 Grolier Multimedia Encyclopedia.* Courtesy, Grolier Interactive, Inc.
21. "New Age music."
22. Martin, p. 61.

Chapter Nine
1. Matthew 5:29–30.
2. Romans 14:13; Romans 14:21; I Corinthians 8:9,12. These verses show the principle that we are to take care not to offend a brother or sister in Christ, nor cause him to stumble. Rock music—including "Christian" rock—has violated this principle by being offensive to many discerning Christians and has caused many others to "stumble" and follow a path destructive to their Christian testimony. (Source: *The Unrecognized Enemy in the Church*, Institute in Basic Life Principles.) Furthermore, little children and new converts are especially vulnerable because of their simple trust that other believers know best. When we, as established believers, allow "Christian" rock music of any sort into the Church, we are giving the children and new converts a

mixed message—a message that compromise is acceptable. Jesus said, *"But whoso shall offend one of these little
ones which believe in me, it were better for him that a mill-
stone were hanged about his neck, and that he were drowned
in the depth of the sea"* (Matthew 18:6; Mark 9:42; Luke
17:2).

3. John 15:18–25.
4. Galatians 5:16.
5. For example: Psalms: 7:17; 9:11; 98:1; 104:33; 105:2;
   108:3; 135:3. Acts 16:25; Ephesians 5:19; Colossians
   3:16; Revelation 15:2–4.
6. Philippians 4:8, paraphrase.
7. Leviticus 11:45; Leviticus 19:2; Luke 1:74–75; II
   Corinthians 7:1; Hebrews 12:14; I Peter 1:15-16; II Peter 3:11.
8. A born-again believer who "walks in the Spirit"
   (Galatians 5:16, 25) need not fear being legalistic. True
   "legalism" is doing a specific list of "works" to gain our
   salvation or, trying to live the Christian life in our own
   energy—*nothing more* (Galatians 2:16; 3:3). If our hearts
   are truly changed, we will *want* to obey God and His
   Word and we should be *praying* to find out how God
   wants us to apply His Word (the Bible) in our lives.

   The "liberty" we have through Christ is merely a
   freedom from *condemnation* and guilt of sin (Romans
   8: 1-3). It is *not* a freedom to live our lives according to
   our own set of values that we blindly claim are approved
   by the Holy Spirit (Galatians 5:13).

   Although the Holy Spirit *has* been given to *"guide
   [us] into all truth"* (John 16:13–14), He will never lead
   us contrary to Scripture. Therefore, it's essential that
   we *know* the Scriptures to discern what is of the Holy
   Spirit and what is *not*.

God may take the same Truth and lead one person
further than another, but the Truth will be valid for both,
and we shouldn't be labeling *anyone* "legalistic" whose
heart's desire is to obey God's leading; rather, we should
respect their commitment.

9. I Corinthians 5:6; Galatians 5:9.
10. II Peter 3:18.
11. Matthew 7:15; Acts 20:29.
12. *chuwl* or *chiyl* (2342), *mechowlah* (4246), *machowl* (4234), Strong, Concordance/Hebrew lexicon, pp. 37 and 64. *orcheomai* (3738), *choros* (5525), Ibid.. Greek lexicon, pp. 52 and 78.
13. Clarence L. Barnhart and Robert K. Barnhart, *The World Book Dictionary*, Vol. Two, p. 1816.
14. *karar* (3769), *raqad* (7540), Strong, Concordance/Hebrew lexicon, pp. 57 and 110.
15. Landeck, p. 133.
16. Galatians 5:17.
17. II Corinthians 5:10.
18. Proverbs 4:23, paraphrase.
19. II Timothy 4:3, paraphrase.
20. From the song, "His Eye Is on the Sparrow," words, Civilla D. Martin; music, Charles H. Gabriel.
21. Romans 14:13; Romans 14:21; I Corinthians 8:9,12. See note number two, this chapter.
22. *Luther's Works*, Volume 53, edited by Ulrich S. Leupold, copyright © 1965 Fortress Press. Used by permission of Augsburg Fortress.
23. Source: David J. De Simone, Religion Historian. Colonial Williamsburg; Williamsburg, VA. NOTE: Even if this was not the case, those original melodies followed Godly principles (i.e., balance and orderliness). Just as an unbeliever may design clothes or, for that matter, anything else we use on a daily basis, if these things

follow Godly principles, they are acceptable for the Christian's use.

24. II Corinthians 6:14.
25. R. M. Longyear, "Music," *The World Book Encyclopedia*, 1989, Vol. 13, p. 958.
26. Abraham, p. 424.
27. Grout, p. 256. NOTE: The use of organ in worship varied according to denomination—even after the seventeenth century and into the eighteenth century.
28. Abraham, p. 436.
29. Ibid., p. 428. NOTE: Although Luther had a great love and appreciation for music (it is said that he "undoubtedly was a musical genius of high rank..."), he was most concerned that the spiritual meaning of the hymns take precedence over the music; in other words, he desired that the music remain uncomplicated. He stated, in a lecture on the psalms, "Psalms and music exist to stimulate the fear of the Lord; when they resound in impure tones, however, they destroy the spirit rather than edify it." Along these same lines, when some church music had become too extravagant, he claimed, "As in the time of King Manasseh the cries of the burning children were drowned out by music and drums, so now church music drowns out the ruin of souls." Resource: Paul Nettl, *Luther and Music*, pp. 62 and 99.
30. Paul Nettl, *Luther and Music*, p. 37.
31. John 6:60-67.
32. Romans 14:11-12; II Corinthians 5:10.

Chapter Ten
1. II Corinthians 6:17, paraphrase.
2. I Peter 2:9.
3. Revelation 3:14–22.
4. Revelation 3:17.

5. I Samuel 16:23.
6. Frank Garlock and Kurt Woetzel, *Music in the Balance*, p. 104.
7. John 4:24; Romans 8:16; I John 5:6–7.
8. Colossians 1:27.
9. Exodus 34:13; Deuteronomy 7:5 (7:1–6); Deuteronomy 12:1–14; Judges 6:25–26; etc.
10. I, personally, have listened to testimonies from different families. Additionally, many other testimonies have been documented in the booklet, *The Unrecognized Enemy in the Church*, available through The Institute in Basic Life Principles, Box One, Oak Brook, IL 60522-3001.

Chapter Eleven
1. Matthew 28:19.
2. Landeck, p. 136.
3. Ibid., p. 13.
4. "Jesus Music" came out of the Jesus Movement, which originated in the mid-1900s on the West Coast of the U.S., then rapidly spread. It was a charismatic Christian movement among young people which combined certain aspects of the young people's lifestyles (rock music) with elements of Pentecostalism. Reference: Walter Holden Capps, "Religion," *The World Book Encyclopedia*, 1989, Vol. 16, p. 226.
5. Some references to light and darkness include: Luke 1:79; Luke 11:34–36; John 1:5; John 3:19–21; John 8:12; John 12:46; Acts 26:18; Romans 13:12; II Corinthians 4:6; II Corinthians 6:14; Ephesians 5:8; Ephesians 5:11; I Thessalonians 5:4–5; I John 1:5.
6. II Corinthians 6:14, NASB.
7. Some references to immoral lifestyles include: Exodus 20:14; Leviticus 20:10; Deuteronomy 5:18; Proverbs

6:32; Matthew 5:27–28; Mark 10:19; I Corinthians 5:9–11; I Corinthians 6:9; I Corinthians 10:8; Galatians 5:19; Ephesians 5:3; Hebrews 13:4.

8. Source: *How to Conquer the Addiction of Rock Music*, Institute in Basic Life Principles.
9. *The American Heritage Dictionary*, p. 154.
10. Taken from *The Ryrie Study Bible*, by Dr. Charles Ryrie. Copyright 1978, p. 1740, Moody Bible Institute of Chicago. Moody Press. Used by permission.
11. I John 1:5.
12. Malachi 3:6; Hebrews 13:8.
13. All four questions are taken from: *The Ryrie Study Bible*, by Dr. Charles Ryrie. Copyright 1978, p. 1740, Moody Bible Institute of Chicago. Moody Press. Used by permission.
14. Refer to endnote number two, chapter nine.
15. Isaiah 61:3.
16. Philippians 4:8, paraphrase.

Chapter Twelve
1. Dr. Charles Stanley, First Baptist Church, Atlanta. Used by permission.
2. Psalms 27:14; 37:34; Isaiah 40:31.
3. I Thessalonians 5:19.
4. Proverbs 3:6.
5. "New": *chadash* (2319), Strong, Concordance/Hebrew lexicon, p. 37. *kainos* (2537), Strong, Concordance/Greek lexicon, p. 39.
6. II Corinthians 6:17, paraphrase.

BIBLIOGRAPHY

Abraham, Gerald, et al. *The Age of Humanism*. Vol. IV of *The New Oxford History of Music*. 1968. By permission of Oxford University Press: New York: London.

Bailey, Albert Edward. *The Gospel in Hymns*. New York: Charles Scribner's Sons, 1950.

Barnhart, Clarence L. and Barnhart, Robert K. *The World Book Dictionary*, Vol. Two. Chicago: World Book, 1989. Used by permission.

Capps, Walter Holden. "Religion." *The World Book Encyclopedia*, 1989, Vol. 16, p. 226.

De Simone, David J. (Religion Historian). Colonial Williamsburg, P.O. Box 1776, Williamsburg, VA 23187. Reference by permission.

Feather, Leonard and Tiegel, Eliot. "Popular music." *The World Book Encyclopedia*, 1989, Vol. 15, p. 673.

Garlock, Frank and Woetzel, Kurt. *Music in the Balance*.* Greenville, SC: Majesty Music, 1992. Used by permission.

"Gospel Music." *The 1995 Grolier Multimedia Encyclopedia*, Compact Disc, Version 7.01. Navato, California: Courtesy, Grolier Interactive, Inc.

Grigadean, Jerry M. "Rock Music." *The World Book Encyclopedia*, 1989, Vol. 16, p. 383.

Groothuis, Douglas R. *Unmasking the New Age.* Downers Grove, Illinois: Intervarsity Press, 1986.

Grout, Donald Jay. *A History of Western Music.* Revised Edition. New York: W. W. Norton and Company, Inc., 1973. Used by permission.

Houghton, S. M. *Sketches from Church History.** Edinburgh, Scotland: Banner of Truth Trust, 1991. Used by permission.

*How to Conquer the Addiction of Rock Music.** Oak Brook, Illinois: Institute in Basic Life Principles, 1993. Reference by permission.

Kirby, F. E. "Classical Music." *The World Book Encyclopedia*, 1989, Vol. 4, p. 647.

Landeck, Beatrice. *Echoes of Africa in Folk Songs of the Americas.** New York: Van Rees Press, 1969.

Longyear, R. M. "Music." *The World Book Encyclopedia*, 1989, Vol. 13, pp. 954-958.

Luther's Works, Volume 53, edited by Ulrich S. Leupold, copyright © 1965 Fortress Press. Used by permission of Augsburg Fortress.

Marrs, Texe. *Dark Secrets of the New Age*. Wheaton, Illinois: Crossway Books, 1987. Used by permission.

Martin, Walter. *The New Age Cult*. Minneapolis: Bethany House, 1989. Used by permission.

Nettl, Paul. *Luther and Music*.* Philadelphia: Fortress Press (formerly Muhlenberg Press), 1948.

"New Age." *The 1995 Grolier Multimedia Encyclopedia*, Compact Disc, Version 7.01. Novato, California: Courtesy, Grolier Interactive, Inc.

"New Age Music." *The 1995 Grolier Multimedia Encyclopedia*, Compact Disc, Version 7.01. Novato, California: Courtesy, Grolier Interactive, Inc.

Peters, Dan and Peters, Steve. *Why Knock Rock?* Minneapolis: Bethany House, 1984.

Ryrie, Charles Caldwell. *The Ryrie Study Bible*, NAS. Copyright 1978, Moody Bible Institute of Chicago. Moody Press. Used by permission.

Smith, Jane Stuart, and Carlson, Betty. *The Gift of Music*.* Wheaton, IL: Crossway Books, 1987. Used by permission.

Stanley, Charles. *How to Listen to God.** Nashville: Oliver-Nelson, 1985. Used by permission.

Strong, James. *The New Strong's Exhaustive Concordance of the Bible*. Nashville: Thomas Nelson, 1984. Used by permission of Thomas Nelson, Inc.

Sykes, James. "Stravinsky, Igor F." *The World Book Encyclopedia*, 1989, Vol. 18, p. 922.

The American Heritage Dictionary. Copyright © 1983 by Houghton Mifflin Company. Adapted and reproduced by permission from *The American Heritage Dictionary, Second Paperback Edition*.

The Unrecognized Enemy in the Church.* Oak Brook, Illinois: Institute in Basic Life Principles, 1990. Reference by permission.

Van Camp, Leonard W. "Hymn." *The World Book Encyclopedia*, 1989, Vol. 9, p. 458.

Van Camp, Leonard W. "Watts, Issac." *The World Book Encyclopedia*, 1989, Vol. 21, p. 149.

Watson, David Lowes. "Wesley, Charles," *The World Book Encyclopedia*, 1989, Vol. 21, p. 198.

Zodhiates, Spiros, Th.D., ed. *The Complete Word Study Dictionary*: New Testament. Revised Edition. Chattanooga, TN: AMG Publishers, 1993. Used by permission.

* Recommended Reading

To order additional copies of

send $9.99 + $3.95 shipping and handling to:

Books, Etc.
PO Box 4888
Seattle, WA 98104

To order by phone,
please have your credit card ready and call

1-800-917-BOOK